Evaluating the Impact of Leadership Coaching

Evaluating the Impact of Leadership Coaching

Balancing immediate performance with longer-term uncertainties

Mark Jamieson and Tony Wall

Open University Press

Open University Press
McGraw Hill
Unit 4,
Foundation Park
Roxborough Way
Maidenhead
SL6 3UD

email: emea_uk_ireland@mheducation.com
www.mheducation.co.uk

A catalogue record of this book is available from the British Library

ISBN-13: 9780335250738
ISBN-10: 0335250734
eISBN: 9780335250745

Library of Congress Cataloging-in-Publication Data
CIP data applied for

Typeset by Transforma Pvt. Ltd., Chennai, India

Praise page

"Does leadership coaching work? Lack of rigorous evaluation has been a major failing of both corporations and the coaching profession. Evaluation is a competence endorsed by all the major professional bodies in coaching, but one that is honoured more in the breach than in practice. So, it's a pleasure to find a comprehensive, insightful and evidence-backed approach with practical examples of how it can be done. Of course, effective coaching isn't about numbers, but it's time to lose the laissez-faire approaches that depict measurement and evaluation as too difficult. Time, indeed, for an upgrade, for which this book provides a valuable foundation."

David Clutterbuck, Special Ambassador, European Mentoring
and Coaching Council

"This book is superbly timely. It brilliantly grasps the difficult and thorny issue of evaluation of coaching and development initiatives in contemporary, uncertain and constantly changing environments. A real aid for leaders, managers and indeed all organizational members.

Jamieson and Wall are supremely well-positioned as authors to write and present this valuable book. Their world class leading-edge approach provides pragmatic yet clear-sighted cutting-edge theory-grounded pathways to address leadership, management and organizational challenges."

Professor Peter Stokes, Leicester Castle Business School,
De Montfort University, UK

"This immensely valuable book provides insightful perspectives about evaluating the impact of leadership coaching. It is based on careful analysis of evidence from different sectors. The book is an excellent quarry of illustrations about pitfalls and opportunities. It introduces the concept of ambidexterity as a valuable lens through which to explore evaluation. It is essential reading for those seeking to ensure that leadership coaching has long term benefits for individuals and organisations."

Professor Peter Shaw, Partner at Praesta Partners (an International
Coaching Organisation), Visiting Professor of Leadership
Development in the UK, Australia, and Canada

"Evaluation remains a key topic for most organisational buyers of leadership coaching. Jamieson and Wall offer a fresh perspective on this old question. Their thesis is models such as ROI fail to acknowledge

the complexity of modern organisational environments and the challenges of measuring human performance, learning and change. 'Evaluating the Impact of Leadership Coaching' makes for a great read from two writers interested in helping move the debate from the facile to the factual, and from ego to evidence."

Prof Jonathan Passmore, Senior VP CoachHub and Professor of
Coaching and Behavioural Change, Henley Business School, UK

"This book offers a much-needed fresh outlook on leadership coaching, particularly focusing on its evaluation (or the lack of it). With a fluent and engaging narrative and a plethora of apt examples in the form of case studies, Mark Jamieson and Tony Wall offer coaches and organizations valuable insights into the process and outcomes of effective evaluation of leadership coaching, presenting evaluation as a strategic opportunity. This is a must-read book for anyone interested or engaged in leadership coaching or any type of coaching in organizations."

Dr Ioanna Iordanou, Reader in Human Resource Management
(Coaching and Mentoring), Oxford Brookes University, UK

"Evaluating the Impact of Leadership Coaching by Mark Jamieson and Tony Wall was a truly fascinating read. I appreciated the candour of the authors in diagnosing the reasons for the lack of evaluation, as well as the discussion as to approaches to overcome the lack of strategic thinking that this represented. Features in the book that were particularly helpful involved the tips and exercises, the chapter tool and template, and the detailed case studies related to different sectors. Although focused on evaluating coaching interventions, this text can be used for supporting any human resource development intervention."

Darlene F. Russ-Eft, Ph.D., Professor Emeritus, Oregon State University,
Assistant Professor of Practice, Purdue University, USA

Dedication

For all those who will remain in our loving memories, as the deepest form of impact.

Professor Tony Wall

Acknowledgements

I would like to take this opportunity to thank my co-author for his teaching and guidance. I would also like to thank Dr Neil Moore for his input to the early stages of research for this book, which could not have been written without the generous encouragement of Dr Ioanna Iordanou. Finally, I would like to thank my personal editor Janine Watson for her patience and skill and, not least, James Jamieson for his emotional and intellectual support.

Dr Mark Jamieson

Contents

List of figures

List of tables

List of case studies

1 Why organizations prioritize leadership coaching and how they are failing to evaluate their investment

Chapter in brief

Since the global financial crisis of 2008, organizations have looked to their leadership to deliver high performance in uncertain times. More recently, the Covid-19 pandemic has proved to be a catalyst for change in the expectations of leadership skills. Therefore, as a result of an increasingly complex leadership landscape, a new set of goals and behaviours have emerged, and the emphasis on intangible soft-skilled targets for leadership has seen coaching become the relied upon development strategy in which organizations have substantially invested. The sizeable investment in coaching corresponds with diminished financial resources and intensifying accountability, naturally placing a spotlight on evaluation. However, evaluation continues to elude organizations as being either too difficult to pursue or limited to uninteresting operational targets. This perplexity is manifest in three paradoxes: despite the strategic emphasis placed upon leadership coaching, evaluation of impact has low strategic status; the coaching outcomes organizations pay for are at odds with evaluation targets; and the evaluation environment is in conflict with valued goals.

Its paradoxical nature sees evaluation: overlooked at a time of intense financial awareness; strategically unambitious at a time of strategic renaissance; and complicit in the non-collaborative relationship between stakeholder and coach provider. This chapter charts the evolution of leadership and leadership coaching, and the apparent failure of evaluation to keep pace.

Introduction

This book sets out to, once and for all, make the case for evaluation, arguing it has been misrepresented as an operational task, when it should be regarded as one of the few remaining untapped strategic resources. Despite its specific focus on leadership coaching, it builds the wider case for evaluation, reimagining it as an essential strategic component of the new organizational mindset. In this opening chapter, we begin by examining the legitimacy of leadership coaching as an organizational strategy, leading to its exponential growth as a business enterprise in its own right, and, despite implicit strategic and explicit operational pressures to do so, the failure to evaluate its impact, as one of the organization's big budget tickets.

As a C-suite director of a private sector company, Mark Jamieson was part of the pioneering organizational executive coaching culture of the 1990s when, certainly for the United Kingdom, coaching was in its infancy as a development strategy. In those days, the very fact that we were using coaches put us ahead of the majority of our competitors, but for the most part, we were flying blind, experimenting with new ideas for talent management. As we and other organizations began to develop a more sophisticated understanding of its potential impact, we began to formalize our relationship with coaching, accumulating sizeable budgets and prioritizing our leadership cohort as the primary focus, to deliver high performance in increasingly competitive markets.

More recently, in his capacity as a practising leadership coach, Mark has a less sanguine view of those days. Yes, we were curious and creative about developing our leaders, but at the same time we made no attempt to be strategically precise or informed as to the impact of either our strategy or our investment; for all we knew, we could have been investing in the emperor's new clothes. At that time, a lack of formal measurement of impact was not considered problematic, despite the implication that its absence downgraded the potential strategic value of the process and closed off a potential source of useful insights into future leadership development programmes; it was enough that we were using coaches.

On reflection, our lack of interest in evaluation was excusable, not only due to the nascency of coaching, but with the transition of leadership thinking at the time. In other words, we did not know what to expect, nor did we know what outcomes we should be evaluating. However, in hindsight, our disinterest in the evaluation of a significant financial investment in a strategic priority, raises some uncomfortable questions about our motives, including: were we committed to leadership coaching as a genuine piece of intelligent strategic thinking, or was coaching actually perceived as a fad, or a marketing ploy to differentiate us from others, in the war to retain and recruit talent (Michaels et al. 2001)?

Over three decades since we started experimenting with coaching, the argument that organizations are flying blind with their coaching investments no longer holds: leadership coaching is an established billion-pound global business, while organizations are knowledgeable and deliberate in the design of leadership dimensions and coaching outcomes, and yet there is compelling evidence to suggest that, with regard to evaluation of impact, we are no further forward.

At a time when resources are limited and financial justification of internal budgets is a day-to-day occupational leadership hazard, we would expect the major investment in coaching should logically place evaluation in the spotlight. However, the relationship between coaching investments and organizational accountability trends is inconsistent and contrary. This tricky relationship is characterized by three paradoxes: despite the strategic emphasis placed upon leadership and leadership coaching, evaluation of impact hardly registers on the executive agenda; when evaluation is attempted, its focus contradicts espoused leadership and coaching outcomes; and those leadership targets organizations state as being valuable, they do not evaluate. These paradoxes are symptomatic of the wider contradictory environment for evaluation, which is: overlooked at a time of intense scrutiny; strategically unambitious when organizations are enjoying a strategic renaissance of high creativity and innovation; and rarely integrated at a time when, it could be argued, coaches and their clients should be working far more collaboratively. To investigate the dysfunctional relationship between leadership coaching and evaluation of impact, we should initially examine why organizations prioritize leadership coaching in the first place, and then investigate their failure to evaluate.

Definitions

There are many definitions of coaching and every coach has their own version. This book would not presume to impose the authors' personal views as to what constitutes a coaching philosophy; however, that being said, it is worth mentioning two fundamental concepts that define the authors' practices (especially as this book relies on a number of illustrative coaching case studies). Firstly, coaching is seen as developmental not remedial, and secondly, the emphasis to deliver valuable outcomes for the client. These foundations for practice are considered to be highly relevant as, collectively, they are the driving force for this book to produce a workable evaluation model.

Similarly, as this book is aimed at coaches (some of whom will be already held in high esteem), the idea of providing a definition for leadership coaching feels unhelpful. However, to enrich the reading experience of the book, it is worth sharing one practice principle – namely, that this form of coaching is highly distinct by being precariously idiosyncratic (Ely et al. 2010). This principle not only informs our practice but was a guiding light when we started to consider the design of a workable evaluation model. Furthermore, what we learnt from researching and writing this book was that we often found the behaviours and mindsets of leadership to overlap (between the coach and the organizational leader) with those of coaching. Despite having to remind ourselves who we were targeting with our theory, this insight encouraged us when testing the transferability of our evaluation model and its potential scope as a wider strategic function.

We should also take time to define the two key components of our book, ambidexterity and evaluation. In the book we make a point of justifying our use of ambidexterity (the capacity of leadership to be adaptive by balancing short-term known and long-term unknown outcomes) as a context for research, due to its overuse as a general cure-all for primary organizational challenges. What we were aiming to achieve was a realistic leadership context in which to research and pilot our model, and we found ambidexterity to be a perfect fit, sharing a number of similar conceptual unknowns with evaluation. Serendipitously, as our work progressed ambidexterity developed into a primary tool, specifically in unlocking the strategic potential of evaluation (possibly reflecting its accurate representation of the current leadership landscape).

Finally, what do we mean by evaluation? At the first level (accountability), evaluation is an assessment of the impact of coaching at accountability and strategic levels. Evaluation is often overlooked because of its connotations with monetizing impact and the concept of return on investment (RoI), which has divided opinion between coaches; some think it is essential while others dismiss it as inappropriate to the coaching methodology. This book argues that evaluation should not be driven by strategically irrelevant financial accountability targets, nor need it be unpalatable to the cultural sensitivities of coaching. It does this by widening the definition of a *return on investment* to serve the individual primary goals of the organization. Therefore, in this book, evaluation is widely defined by the diverse needs of the individual client, which may include intangible RoI goals such as behaviours, well-being, social and potential. This broader scope for RoI allows evaluation to be seen as two-dimensional and stresses its function, at the second level, as a strategic informant. It is our aim that our final evaluation model be defined by its ability to work in concert with both accountability and strategic functions.

Tips and exercises 1

Tip   *Our histories with coaching and forms of learning evaluation shape the way we see the possibilities for coaching evaluation. It is useful to be aware of this so that we can address our blind spots and expand creative possibilities in and through our own practice.*

Reflective exercise   What is your history with coaching? For example, how were you introduced to it? Who introduced you? What has coaching given you (or not) in the past?

What was coaching used for when you first experienced it, and how has it changed since, in your experience?

What might these reflections tell you about how you see coaching and its function in your work today?

A new leadership mindset made for coaching

Since the global financial crisis of 2008 (GFC), leadership has been designated strategic priority status as organizations strive to survive and thrive in uncertain times and ever more competitive marketplaces. This level of financial precariousness has been exacerbated by the Covid-19 pandemic, which has added cultural pressures to leadership as organizations react to the changed workplace needs of their people. Emerging from a dynamic and complex operating environment, leadership has evolved and a new set of expectations has been identified, emphasizing unfamiliar, soft-skill intangible targets, within the domain of the coaching methodology. Accordingly, leadership coaching has become the relied upon development strategy, into which organizations are prepared to invest considerable sums of money.

The business case for leadership coaching is widely evidenced in numerous practice surveys specifically focused on global leadership trends (CIPD 2011, 2015, 2017; DDI 2018; ICF 2014). We have captured the headline findings from this research, in the dichotomy: organizations with the highest quality of leadership outperform their competitors; at a time when most organizations report, they do not have confidence that their leadership is equipped to tackle the challenges of an increasingly complex operating environment. Additionally, there is also evidence that organizations acknowledge the dominant determinant of leadership effectiveness lies in the quality of their leadership development strategies. Having put two and two together, the challenge for organizations is where and how to invest in the development of their leadership. To do this, they need to clearly define the critical outcomes they require and seek out the most effective methods available to them in an overcrowded marketplace aggressively competing for their attention.

Tips and exercises 2

Tip	*The written documents linked to coaching often reveal the explicit or implied reason for it. These can reveal indicators as to the form and focus of evaluation, but also potential conflicts, tensions, and also blind spots as to what evaluation could address.*
Reflective exercise	Gather written documents about coaching in your organization, or the coaching you deliver. What can you learn about how it is perceived or used in your work? What are the themes or patterns in the problems or priorities it seeks to address?

A review of the literature around that time (post GFC) provides a general consensus of opinion, confirming organizations were seeking a new direction from their leadership to lead them to recovery and beyond. The GFC is considered a watershed moment for most organizations; however, the change in thinking about the direction of leadership was not the result of a single economic event. It was the accumulation of a number of circumstances including simultaneous political, global, technological and demographic shifts, exacerbated by the Covid-19 pandemic, that shaped the workplace and attitudes to work, from which emerged the new criteria for leadership. The subsequent repositioning of leadership to accommodate a new set of outcomes meant the development of unfamiliar behaviours and ways of thinking based on experiential and emotional behavioural science, and the growing influence of evolving attitudes and beliefs. As part of the fallout from the evolution of leadership, it was also recognized that organizations would be challenged to dismantle existing hierarchies and re-examine their relationship with leadership effectiveness, now characterized, in the broadest terms, by the ability to change, learn and take calculated risks. What business strategists refer to as organizational agility.

We should state that organizational agility has been around for some time and was not suddenly conceived as a response to the GFC. In 2005, Erickson and Dyer defined it as the ability to purposefully adapt behaviours and systems in response to external (economic, political, technological, global and demographic) disruptions, by moving seamlessly in multiple directions. This definition (one of many) fits perfectly with our own understanding and provides us with a developable conceptual basis for ideas later in the book. The pursuit of agility has exposed traditional leadership development targets as being outdated. Accordingly, these have now been superseded by a new set of seemingly counter-intuitive goals and competencies, focused on long-term intangible behaviours, reflecting the shift in emphasis that recognizes purpose (as a long-term goal) as well as profit (as a short-term target), or specifically: managing the tension between financial risk (for profit) and cultural risk (for future relevance). In doing so, organizations are being invited to consider longer-term influencers such as culture and values, as they move away from short-term opportunism, in the design of the new leadership landscape.

As a subtext, organizations are also working on the theory that high performance is embedded in their people resource, which, in turn, is dependent on superior methods of leadership to motivate talent. High performance levels and talent management have been considered a marriage of convenience for time immemorial, and focusing on recruitment and retention of stars is hardly a new phenomenon (Michaels et al. were coining the phrase 'war for talent' at the turn of this century). However, it is fair to say that technological advancement, strategic mergers resulting in dominant behemoths, and increasingly creative (and highly financially supported) marketing initiatives have refocused the organization on their human resource, as the fine line between success and failure, as the so-called war for talent enters a new phase.

The drive for marketable differentiation is accompanied by an emerging generation as the new primary workforce (it is estimated that by 2025 millennials will comprise 75 per cent of the global workforce), which has focused leadership on different recruitment incentives and new ideas for the development of talent. Therefore, in rethinking leadership outcomes, organizations are also heeding the research into how millennials want to work and live (Gallup 2016): purpose over pay; personal development over job satisfaction; ongoing assessments over annual reviews; developmental (of strengths) over remedial (fixing weaknesses); coaching over managing. It is also clear that the coronavirus pandemic will also greatly impact the way different generations perceive work, accelerating change in an unforgiving timescale to challenge the leaders of today. As we begin to recharacterize the relationship between leadership and coaching, we might posit the emergence of the manager-coach, implying that today's leadership is expected to bear the responsibility of inspiring and motivating the people they lead by adopting coaching behaviours which, either by design or coincidence, aligns directly to all items on the aforementioned millennial wish list.

Recent research from the Chief Learning Officer Business Intelligence Board (Prokopeak 2018) supports the claim that the dimensions of coaching and leadership are moving ever closer together, revealing how organizations are in transition, shifting towards a new set of leadership development goals focused on succession, retention, creativity and innovation, and culture. And additional data reveals that, with regard to the skills targeted for frontline leadership, coaching is placed ahead of communication, business acumen, employee engagement and critical thinking.

Reflecting the increasing overlap between leadership and coaching, the nature of shared outcomes, and the shift in mindset and behaviours being asked of leaders to deliver them, unsurprisingly, organizations have turned to coaching as the natural-fit development strategy for their leadership cohorts. Inevitably, leadership coaching has become big business in its own right. The Chief Learning Officer Business Intelligence Board (Prokopeak 2018) estimates that nearly 95 per cent of organizations either plan to maintain or increase their investment in leadership coaching, while estimates of between $50 billion and $366 billion monetized leadership development as a global industry in 2018.

Further evidence that the direction of organizational financial firepower has turned upon leadership development through coaching is implied by the corresponding underinvestment in employee training (CIPD 2018, 2020) where, conversely, organizations are investing less in this area than they did 20 years ago, despite acknowledging that 'skills and capabilities of the workforce are vital to economic sustainability and growth'. Insightful as it is, the Chartered Institute of Personnel and Development's (CIPD) point of view is arguably one-dimensional, focusing on a strategic response to diminishing resources and increasingly competitive marketplaces. Therefore, it does not factor in the new expectations placed upon leaders to develop and coach their teams, as a determinant for the fall in training investment and the notion that coaching behaviours are now a leadership coaching outcome in themselves, which implies the organization now sees employee development as an internal responsibility for the leader.

Failing to evaluate: looking beyond *how?* to *why?*

Only time will tell whether a highly disproportionate focus on leadership coaching over employee training is the right strategy for the current period. What is now clear is that organizations have made a leap of faith by going for broke, investing in their leaders and, in doing so, rewriting the leader's job description, the expectations of which are perfectly aligned to coaching as a development strategy. As an unexpected consequence, it can be argued that coaching and leadership dimensions have begun to merge and there is a legitimate requirement for them to become interchangeable in the line of leadership responsibilities. What is less clear is why organizations are failing to evaluate their significant investment in a primary strategy.

From our recent research (Jamieson, Wall and Moore 2020), the following quotation from the Director of People and Change at a large government department encapsulated the paradoxical nature of evaluation:

> *We know what we expect from our leaders but that's not what we evaluate. Evaluation is focused on operational outcomes; critical frontline measures on people: normal HR stuff – but nothing that deals with the causes, or is strategically focused. We know there's a gap, but I can't explain why.*

Evidence suggests that the idea of evaluation continues to elude, both practically and intellectually, organizations and coaches alike. In 2015 the CIPD produced research that spotlighted the organizational struggle to evaluate the impact of their leadership coaching investments as part of a strategically aligned process. In summarizing their findings, they concluded:

- One in seven organizations make no attempt to evaluate in any shape or form.
- Over a third of organizations limit their evaluation to anecdotal evidence based on the satisfaction levels of those taking part.
- Only one in five organizations try to assess the impact of coaching in the workplace.
- Only a small minority of organizations evaluate the wider impact on business or society.

Similar themes were uncovered by a European Mentoring and Coaching Council (EMCC) Provocations Report (Wall et al. 2017), providing a coach perspective for a 360-degree view of attitudes to evaluation. This research used a small international sample of 13 leadership coaches to explore evaluation across three main themes: *how?* (method), *why?* (motive), *what?* (targets). Its findings completed the picture for current evaluation practice, supporting the headline findings from the CIPD:

- Around 25 per cent of coaches made no attempt to evaluate, claiming: it was not their place; there was no organizational evaluation culture; evaluation (specifically financial) was not appropriate for their coaching ethics.
- When specifically questioned about how evaluation was undertaken, all coaches said they used a standardized participation satisfaction survey. At best, these required the leadership coachee to respond by providing a written piece of reflection on the effects of the coaching. More often, the coaching effectiveness was evaluated using a Likert scale (1–10) with questions such as: Would you recommend me? To what extent were outcomes achieved?
- When specifically questioned about what they evaluated, coaches more often referred to Kirkpatrick's four-level evaluation model (1959a, 1959b), specifically levels 1 and 2 (self-assessed satisfaction and peer-assessed behavioural change). A small minority of respondents did refer to Kirkpatrick's level 4 (results), but these were limited to self-serving purposes designed to prove coaching efficacy (and therefore unreliable as an organizational weathervane for future leadership strategies).
- When specifically questioned about why evaluation took place, participants referred to a diverse set of motives, including justification for the coaching engagement, marketing for a continuing engagement, and quality assurance.

Figure 1: Organizational and coaching perspectives for attitudes to evaluation

Organizational perspective for attitudes to evaluation	Coaching perspective for attitudes to evaluation
1 in 7 make no attempt to evaluate	Around 25% of coaches make no attempt to evaluate
Over a third limit evaluation to anecdotal evidence	All coaches used a standardized evaluation self-assessment form requiring varying degrees of client reflection
1 in 5 attempt to assess the impact of coaching in the workplace	A small minority attempt to assess impact for self-serving motives
A small minority evaluate the wider impact	None mentioned the wider impact

The evidence is irrefutable, then: organizations and coaches have a blind spot when it comes to effective evaluation. A number of scholars and practitioners have contributed insights into how evaluation eludes the evaluation stakeholder, with much of the focus on the practical challenges faced. Later, this book will go on to mythologize these challenges and the self-fulfilling belief that they are insurmountable but, in the meantime, it is worth providing the reader with a snapshot of them now, as a record of current thinking, and an entry point to the more subtle, undetected intellectual barriers that organizations face.

In 2014, the International Coaching Federation (ICF) asserted that time, budget and ability were the most reported barriers to evaluation for organizations using leadership coaches. More recently, the EMCC research (Wall et al. 2017) provided a refined view of evaluation challenges, claiming that organizations were generally taxed by contingencies, intangibles and strategic alignment. This represented a more complex set of challenges, reflecting the ongoing shift from an operational to an increasingly strategically focused organizational perspective. A thumbnail sketch of these now provides a helpful introduction to some of the fundamental ideas in the next two chapters.

Firstly, contingencies, which are characterized as the complexity resulting from meta-trends: political and economic volatility; globalization; technological advancement and shifting demographics (especially generational changes in the workplace). As a result, it is accepted that leadership outcomes have become a moving target as organizations grapple with external forces and internal evolution. Secondly, intangibles, reflecting emerging unconventional and non-traditional leadership goals that emphasize the idiosyncratic nature of both coaching and leadership. Here, organizations have struggled to isolate the impact of soft-skills and elicit meaningful comparisons with tangible targets for evaluation. Finally, strategic alignment, referring to multiple definitions and conceptual ambiguity of what constitutes value. Historically, this has perplexed evaluation practitioners because of diverse organizational goals and multiple stakeholders with different motivations, rendering definitions of value vulnerable to inconsistency and ambiguity through stakeholder subjectivity.

What is clear from a review of the considerable weight of literature in this field is that there is no shortage of opinion or understanding about how organizations and coaches are finding evaluation problematic. At the same time, it is equally apparent from the practice surveys and evaluation practitioner's attitudes that, despite an outpouring of knowledge and theory, very little progress has been made. Wall et al. (2016) investigated this lack of progress, producing an insightful report that flagged the potential issues for evaluation arising from the gap between theory and practice, arguing that organizations are not heeding research because it is unrelatable, overly complex and inaccessible. And a second school of thought claims that researchers themselves should shoulder much of the blame by being too shallow in their outlook, adopting a narrow or one-dimensional perspective, assuming the organization's preoccupation with operational HR targets or future programme design. As part of this thinking, it is suggested, this apparent lack of ambition for evaluation is off-putting to practitioners as they can see no strategic relevance (and therefore, no incentive) to invest time and money in the design of an evaluation system. Either way, the gap between theory and practice suggests the reason organizations are failing to evaluate their leadership coaching investments is as much intellectual as it is practical.

The preoccupation with the evaluation as a conundrum to produce a workable system means the question that rarely gets asked is *why* organizations and coaches are intellectually disengaged with evaluation. Therefore, having established *how* organizations struggle practically to use evaluation, we now turn to those intellectual factors that demotivate stakeholders and practitioners. In doing so, three key areas emerged from our research: end goals (destination of evaluation data); culture (the values and philosophy of the brand); and strategic disconnect (the internal context and the tension between operational and strategic factions).

End goals

Our research (Wall et al. 2017; Jamieson, Wall and Moore 2020) revealed that it is not wholly the tricky nature of evaluation that deters practitioners, but its perceived limitations, specifically, the destination of evaluation data. Unsurprisingly, as organizational leadership development strategies focused on creative and innovative behavioural and mindset changes, a strategically unambitious evaluation offering has scant relevance. Jamieson, Wall and Moore (2020) produce further evidence of the trend for organizations to be strategically timid with evaluation. Figure 2 summarizes the responses from 12 senior organizational evaluation stakeholders when specifically questioned about evaluation data collection and data usage in their individual organizations. The research found that four destination categories for resultant data emerged: reward and recognition; programme maintenance; operational; and strategic.

Figure 2: Summary of responses of key stakeholders towards evaluation (Jamieson, Wall and Moore 2020)

Remuneration	75%
Progress	75%
Programme	40%
Design	75%
Advocacy	30%
Continuation	30%
Talent group	5%
Social impact	10%
Organizational change	5%
Well-being	15%
Funding	40%
Communication	5%
Diversity	30%
HR targets	15%

	Reward and recognition
	Programme maintenance
	Strategic
	Operational

Tips and exercises 3

Tip   *It is useful to get a sense of the reasons for coaching evaluation, and this can be done easily through conversation or through a quick group or team survey.*

Reflective   Based on your observations and experiences of coaching in your
exercise   organization, or an organization you coach for or with, what would
              you say are the top three reasons that explain why **leadership coaching** evaluation is conducted?

Remuneration
Progress
Programme
Design
Advocacy
Continuation
Talent group
Social impact
Organizational change
Well-being
Funding
Communication
Diversity
HR targets

What about the reasons for **other coaching** activity? Rank the top three reasons:

Remuneration
Progress
Programme
Design
Advocacy
Continuation
Talent group
Social impact
Organizational change
Well-being
Funding
Communication
Diversity
HR targets

If there are differences, what has happened in the organization's history which might explain these differences?

If there are differences, what is it in the organization's climate or culture which might explain these differences?

Now, what are *your* reasons for evaluating leadership coaching? Rank your top three reasons:

Remuneration
Progress
Programme
Design
Advocacy
Continuation
Talent group
Social impact
Organizational change
Well-being
Funding
Communication
Diversity
HR targets

When you take the above reflections together, what might this tell you about possible tensions or conflicts in perspective, or possible blind spots in practice?

One interpretation is that organizations are motivated to evaluate when they have a clear end goal for the destination of data. The graphic (Figure 2) shows that the dominant categories, reward and recognition, and programme maintenance are monetarily focused, often determined by the sector type (For Profit or For Purpose), performing necessary financial tasks for compensation or budgetary justification. However, although this illustrates that organizations are somewhat engaged with evaluation, it also brings to life the three evaluation paradoxes: despite the strategic emphasis placed upon leadership and leadership coaching, evaluation appears to be of little strategic interest; when evaluation is attempted, its focus contradicts espoused organizational and coaching outcomes; and those outcomes organizations say they value, they do not evaluate.

An alternative perspective for the idea that financially focused end goals motivate and simultaneously limit evaluation occurred when respondents in both (organizational and coaching) categories of research reported evaluation as being assumed or incidental. A director from an international bank:

It's very hard to evaluate leadership coaching impact, because without coaching we would undoubtedly accomplish a lot; we just believe that with the openness and focus coaching brings, we will accomplish more.

Perhaps of more concern is the subtext beneath the headline and the tendency for these organizations to turn to evaluation as an afterthought. In these instances, organizations only became aware of evaluation, superficially in terms of accountability, when their bottom line was underperforming.

Culture

It is apparent that culture is a significant influence on attitudes to evaluation. When interviewed, stakeholders and practitioners generally spoke about culture in terms of ethics, values and philosophy. The senior partner from a private sector firm put it this way:

We are an old-fashioned partnership built on principles of 'Trust, Know and Respect'. Decisions are made based on these principles, it is hardly scientific – rightly or wrongly – but it's how we work. A whole string of KPIs [key performance indicators] for evaluation just would not be appropriate.

At the same time, the tone of some of the responses from coaches reflected a high level of sensitivity, almost to the extent that offence had been taken at the very thought of evaluation, especially where return on investment was considered as synonymous:

Where there is emphasis on monetizing coaching interventions, to tell the truth, I refuse this kind of job, because this does not complement my style of coaching and is an inappropriate measure.

Strategic disconnect

Finally, we found evidence of a strategic disconnect between operational (HR) and strategic (executive) functions. This evaluation tension is covered in detail later in the book; however, suffice to say, we thematically found evidence of the organization's capability to conspire against itself, not connecting operational and strategic functions, to fail to evaluate effectively. In some of the most extreme cases, this was manifest as a deliberate blocking tactic from the operational HR stakeholder for the dissemination of potentially strategically useful data. Furthermore, strategic disconnect was found to occur when the internal context produced an unhelpful environment for evaluation, either through self-serving reward and recognition systems, or inconsistency and bias from an impartial evaluator.

Leadership coaching and high performance are now a major strategic connection and, in an environment where uncertainty has become normalized and the workplace is in transition, there is every reason this relationship will continue to blossom. At the same time, commentators have reported that evaluation is at a crossroads and organizations need to take it seriously – the only problem being, this is not a new message and evaluation has been talked about in this vein since the GFC 2008, with organizations continuing to fail to effectively evaluate one of their most significant investments.

Having introduced some traditional and some new ideas about how organizations are failing to evaluate, the next chapter recreates the complex organizational context to put these to the test, to find out if the problematic nature of evaluation is actually a self-fulfilling prophecy by which organizations and coaches are condemned to fail, or whether it can be reimagined as a strategic boon.

Summary of key points

Organizations look to leadership to deliver adaptive strategies for high performance in complex markets. Accordingly, leadership has evolved and a new set of expectations, shaped by a dynamic environment and a seismic generational shift in the workplace, has seen the exponential growth of leadership coaching as the relied upon development solution. However, despite the high investment (financially and strategically), organizations have low expectation of evaluation, which takes place in a paradoxical environment, perceived as an operational task and strategically unambitious. From recent research, three key areas have emerged as reasons given for the apparent lack of interest shown in evaluation: end goals, culture and strategic disconnect. These provide valuable new insights, updating conventional thinking around evaluation barriers, refocusing attention on intellectual rather than practical blind spots, moving the focus away from *how?* we fail to evaluate, to *why?*

Chapter tool/template

Tool (for personal practice):

Why evaluate (personal reflection)

Reflecting on the reasons to assess is a helpful tool to judge the perceived function and value of coaching evaluation at any level.

A simple set of questions with individuals, groups or teams can include:

- What will we do with the findings of our evaluation?
- What do we want our evaluation to do for us?

There may be times when you need to support the individual, team or group to articulate the rationale, so a ranking survey can help. For example:

What are the top three reasons for this/our evaluation? List the first, second and third in order of importance (first being most important):

Remuneration
Progress
Programme
Design
Advocacy
Continuation
Talent group
Social impact
Organizational change
Well-being
Funding
Communication
Diversity
HR targets

Template: Why evaluate?

What are the top three reasons for this/our evaluation? List the first, second and third in order of importance (first being most important):

Remuneration
Progress
Programme
Design
Advocacy
Continuation
Talent group
Social impact
Organizational change
Well-being
Funding
Communication
Diversity
HR targets

2 How ambidexterity awarded strategic thinking an *A+* and exposed evaluation as a *Fail*

Chapter in brief

Research approaches have in part been blamed for the lack of progress made in the field of evaluation, specifically the failure to develop theory in a real-life context. This chapter introduces organizational ambidexterity (the capacity of leadership to be adaptive by balancing short-term-known and long-term-unknown outcomes) to replicate the current dynamic leadership environment, and as a context to study evaluation. In doing so, it reveals two main headlines: ambidexterity is welcomed by organizations as a seedbed for creative and innovative strategies for high performance; and, on closer examination, the characteristics of ambidexterity begin to cast doubt on our assumptions about conventional problematics (contingencies, intangibles and strategic align-ment). We convert the concept of ambidexterity into a strategic tool, producing a conceptual framework as a reference point for an examination of existing organizational strategies.

Employing three mini case studies, we illustrate how organizations posi-tively embrace ambidexterity as a leadership strategy, using frameworks as either operational or conceptual balance mechanisms, connecting counter-intuitive intangible leadership outcomes to tangible targets by placing them in the context of a primary goal, or integrating them within internal appraisal systems. We then go on to question why these frameworks are not extended to include evaluation, providing anecdotal evidence supporting superficial find-ings from the previous chapter that practitioners resort to end goals, culture and strategic disconnect as an explanation for disregarding evaluation, which is treated as either a task or an inconvenience.

Introduction

In the previous chapter, we posited the notion that researchers and practitioners were failing to make progress in this area because of a preoccupation with *how?* we failed to evaluate (in essence, re-proving what we already know about barriers) rather than *why?* In doing so, we implied that the trouble with evaluation was not solely a practical conundrum to be solved, but an intellectual puzzle based on motives, attitudes and the strategic mindset. Redirecting our gaze in this way provides the energy for this book, to see evaluation, not just as a problem to be solved, but as a strategic opportunity at a time of confusion, complexity and change. Our starting point to get to *why* was to close the gap between theory and practice by responding to criticism that researchers in this field do not formulate their ideas in a real-life context. In this chapter, we set out to recreate the complex organizational environment, within which today's leaders are expected to operate, as a stage to test existing theories and new ideas. To achieve this, we introduce the reader to organizational ambidexterity (the capacity of leadership to be adaptive by balancing short-term-known and long-term-unknown outcomes) as representative of the current leadership context and the challenge to be strategically agile.

Using a lens of ambidexterity to examine the relationship between leadership, leadership coaching and evaluation, revealed two seminal headlines: organizations actually embraced the challenges of a volatile operating environment, treating it as a springboard for creative and innovative solutions; and ambidexterity was found to negate perceived evaluation barriers, opening up not only practical design dimensions, but also suggesting a wider role as a strategic function. Serendipitously, our chosen context for research was found to be a strategic catalyst for leadership and coaching, simultaneously neutralizing those elements reported to hinder evaluation. The fact that organizations already had the incentive and the wherewithal to make evaluation work for them, but that this lay buried in their subconscious, supported our assertion that evaluation inhibition is largely in the mind and, therefore, a far more complex challenge than previously thought.

A word about ambidexterity and how we chose it

What we knew was that organizations now strive for agility, and look to their leadership to deliver creative adaptive strategies, balancing the immediate day-to-day imperatives for survival with long-term projects that will ensure they thrive beyond recovery. What we needed was to replicate a real-life leadership environment as a context for our investigations. What we needed to avoid was a generalized, broad-brush description of a complex leadership landscape, a proven limiter of new knowledge for researchers. What we wanted to do was to bring to life today's leadership challenges in a way that was relevant and instantly relatable, recognizing the evolving leadership mindset identified in the previous chapter.

Tips and exercises 4

Reflective exercise When you hear, read or think of the idea of 'ambidexterity', what comes to mind? In everyday use of the word, we may think of using both our left and right hands with equal fluency. What images does it conjure up in relation to your leadership or coaching work?

Organizational ambidexterity is not a new idea. In 1991, March asserted that, to be adaptive, organizations needed to simultaneously exploit current capabilities and existing assets, while intentionally making time for exploration of new ideas for future competitive relevance. In 2004, O'Reilly and Tushman developed the concept, describing the ability to achieve game-changing innovations at the same time as tweaking the existing business for steady improvements, as a battleground of leadership thought. Although we felt this was a good contextual fit for this book, we, in turn, have refined and updated the concept, specifically to make it more accessible and relevant to both leaders and readers. Accordingly, terms such as exploitative and explorative have been given a wider context to encompass short-term, known, tangible targets (exploitative) and long-term, unknown, intangible goals (explorative). Finally, we were attracted to the pivotal role of leadership to deliver ambidextrous strategies, accepting the leader as the key stakeholder for the diverse and competing needs of the organization.

Tips and exercises 5

Tip *Ambidexterity is about the use of limited resource to balance the needs of a known-now with a future unknown scenario: balancing the need to deliver operationally now and to build new capability for an uncertain future.*

We also wanted to safeguard the integrity of this book, aware of criticism that ambidextrous strategies are overused and, often, a lazy research option to solve most primary organizational challenges. Satisfied this was the real-life leadership scenario for which we were looking, we found a number of common themes with evaluation that enhanced its credentials. These included: unique interpretations across organizational sectors (we were particularly interested in distinct attitudes from different sectors for transferable knowledge); positive strategic connotations (strategic potential in the case of evaluation) and the influence of the internal organizational context. Furthermore, the unresolved issues with ambidexterity also resonated with us, as being similar to those of evaluation, including: simplistic definitions (neither are understood in convenient binary terms); indeterminate timelines, and ambiguity arising from subjective interpretations. Lastly, we felt that the approach to ambidextrous outcomes as separate exploitative and explorative constructs, emphasizing measurable exploitative targets, mirrored current attitudes to evaluation and would support our pursuit of a possible, harmonic strategy.

A word on our research sample

This book revolves around leadership. Unsurprisingly, we deliberately limited our primary research sample (Jamieson, Wall and Moore 2020) to 12 current organizational C-suite decision-makers with the ultimate say over leadership coaching strategies (rather than a larger group focused on the operational side of human resource development). We also drew on interviews with 13 international leadership coaches (Wall et al. 2017) as part of an earlier research project for the EMCC. We conducted a series of in-depth semi-structured interviews with the first group, asking them about their experiences of evaluation in the context of ambidexterity in terms of judgements, barriers and the potential benefits of a practical framework that connected evaluation to strategy. Our interviews with the second group explored evaluation experiences in diverse practice landscapes, providing us with multiple perspectives for a complete picture.

Introducing ambidexterity as a lens through which to explore evaluation

As a part of the process to unpack the concept of organizational ambidexterity, we designed our own ambidextrous framework to graphically replicate the current leadership environment (Table 1). Our aim was to produce a framework from a synthesis of existing knowledge (taken from an extensive review of current literature) that was also practically familiar to our research participants. In formulating this framework, we wanted to characterize leadership as a decision-making process, accommodate emergent coaching targets and link these to evaluation. In doing so, we paid particular attention to detail, especially in the wording and tone. This enabled us to use it as a visual reference point throughout the process of data collection, where it was vital, not least for the credibility of the research, that discussions were conducted in a language that was both recognizable and relevant to the interviewee.

Table 1 The conceptual framework for ambidextrous decision-making used in our research

Exploitative ambidextrous characteristics: short-term – known outcomes	Explorative ambidextrous characteristics: long-term – unknown outcomes	Ambidextrous balance proposition	Emergent leadership coaching ambidextrous dimensions from the literature to develop approaches for:	Implications for dimensions of evaluation
Financial risk[a] pressing business imperatives with strong financial legitimacy	Cultural risk[a] long-term vision through innovation, creativity and capacity building with weak financial legitimacy	Performance versus future competitive relevance	Managing risk[a]	Balancing performance with competitive relevance in the context of managing risk
Respond – operate in a complex[b] but known environment	Anticipate – operate in a complex[b] but unknown environment	Complex environment versus opportunity generation	Managing change[c]	Balancing a complex environment with opportunity generation in the context of managing change
Scalability[d]	Capacity building[e]	Efficiency savings versus talent management for pivotal high-impact roles	Managing multiple conflicting structures and systems[e]	Balancing efficiency savings with talent management for pivotal roles in the context of managing multiple structures
Allocation of resources to areas of high impact[e, f]	Allocation of resources to areas of future development[e, f]	Budgetary justification versus culture of collective understanding	Strategic alignment[g]	Balancing internal budgetary justification with a culture of collective understanding in the context of managing strategic alignment
Recruitment and retention[h]	Succession[i]	Management versus leadership	Social integration and relationship management – talent management[j]	Balancing management with leadership perspectives in the context of managing social integration and relationships

(Continued)

Table 1 (Continued)

Exploitative ambidextrous characteristics: short-term – known outcomes	Explorative ambidextrous characteristics: long-term – unknown outcomes	Ambidextrous balance proposition	Emergent leadership coaching ambidextrous dimensions from the literature to develop approaches for:	Implications for dimensions of evaluation
Cost – training[k]	Investment – coaching[k]	RoI versus well-being and engagement Coaching efficacy versus awareness of fuller range of coaching outcomes	Professional judgement[l]	Balancing RoI with well-being and engagement in the context of managing professional judgement Balancing coaching efficacy with a fuller range of coaching outcomes

a Beer 2015; Thunnissen, Boselie and Fruytier 2013.
b Hatum 2010.
c Ely et al. 2010; Hall, Otazo and Hollenbeck 1999.
d Ericksen and Dyer 2005.
e Cappelli 2008; Fernandez-Araoz, Groysberg and Nohria 2011; Lepak and Shaw 2008; McDonnell 2011; O'Reilly and Tushman 2013; Wright and McMahan 2011.
f Yapp 2009.
g CIPD 2014.
h Cappelli 2008; Michaels, Handfield-Jones and Axelrod 2001.
i Ely et al. 2010.
j Hatum 2010; Lewis and Heckman 2006; Skillings 2008.
k Angrave et al. 2016; Becker, Huselid and Beatty 2009; Kaufman 2015; Thunnissen, Boselie and Fruytier 2013; Wright and McMahan 2011.
l Wall et al. 2017.

Tips and exercises 6

Tip   *The notion of a 'balance' (or equilibrium) has become popular as a way to indicate 'health' in all aspects of business and life – a balanced diet, work–life balance, everything in moderation (the Goldilocks principle of 'not too much, not too little'). This is not a new concept – we can see evidence symbolized in ancient oriental thought as ying–yang, or as the appreciation of opposites in ancient Greek civilizations.*

This table shows the effect of applying a strategic context: sharpening the focus for organizational goals and leadership targets; breaking down the dominant challenge for leaders to make balanced and complex decisions between short- and long-term priorities. The framework provides a visual explanation of, not only the current leadership context, but the evolution of leadership goals, providing definition to the assumptions, generalizations and oversimplifications that have characterized many previous studies. From here, a leadership landscape emerges, specifically focused on the facilitation of change in areas of: goal setting (managing risk); strategic agility (managing change); strategic prioritization (managing internal structural conflict); strategic alignment; talent management, and leadership judgement. At the same time, ambidexterity has begun to untangle the mystery of leadership coaching, referred to by Ely and colleagues (2010) as its idiosyncratic nature, providing the coach, and latterly the evaluation process, with clear targets for emotional, cognitive and behavioural development, as well as more conventional, technical support. As a result, it can be claimed, the focus for leadership coaching is now much more precise, albeit multidimensional, the outcomes of which combine tangible targets and intangible goals along variable timelines.

Tips and exercises 7

Tip   *Coaches are very familiar with the implications and constraints of binary thinking: 'either–or'. Binaries can also be productive cognitive devices to help us attempt to identify particular thinking or behavioural patterns, and to provoke new possibilities and choices. Ambidexterity – and the propositions presented in this book – are intentionally used in the same way, to help provoke awareness and choice for a longer-term view.*

Reflective   The six balance propositions, from the table above, are:
exercise
                1 Balancing performance with competitive relevance in the context of managing risk
                2 Balancing a complex environment with opportunity generation in the context of managing change

---

3 Balancing efficiency savings with talent management for pivotal roles in the context of managing multiple structures
4 Balancing internal budgetary justification with a culture of collective understanding in the context of managing strategic alignment
5 Balancing management with leadership perspectives in the context of managing social integration and relationships
6 Balancing RoI with well-being and engagement in the context of managing professional judgement
7 Balancing coaching efficacy with a fuller range of coaching outcomes

What are your initial reflections and reactions to these propositions? Are any immediately familiar or surprising?

Thinking about the leadership team of an organization you have worked for, or are currently working for, which of the propositions were *most* and *least* present in your engagement in that team from your proposition perspective?

Most present:

Least present:

Having met our primary objective, adopting and applying ambidexterity as a context or lens for exploring evaluation, we were surprised to subsequently discover that, despite its complexities, ambidexterity was being actively used by organizations as a strategic opportunity to deliver an agile and adaptive environment. Our conceptual framework was found to accurately reflect the real-life experiences of leadership decision-making and our participants were able to apply their individual versions of the process of making connections across the six suggested coaching dimensions. In short, organizations were using a complex environment to pursue innovative and creative strategies, driven by leadership, through various iterations of ambidextrous models already in place.

How organizations are using ambidextrous frameworks as a strategic springboard

We found organizations were using ambidextrous frameworks as balance mechanisms for leadership decision-making, systematically laying out a strategic road map to assist leaders in exercising good judgement through prioritizing key decisions in the right order. Let us firstly explain the concept of balance mechanisms.

Balance mechanisms

A balance mechanism is an ambidextrous system, usually a framework, used by the organization to set out expectations for leaders, and by placing these in the context of a primary goal (profit, performance or purpose) provides a set of criteria against which performance can be judged. Organizations use two types of balance mechanism: operational and conceptual, normally in isolation, but sometimes in conjunction with each other.

Operational balance mechanisms

Operational balance mechanisms are focused on improving leadership performance by increasing the effectiveness of day-to-day leadership tasks. They take the form of a generic (to the organization) framework or model, clearly identifying outcomes, targets and goals, thereby streamlining working practice by sharpening the leader's focus on a primary goal (the principal business of the organization). We found various examples of operational balance mechanisms reflecting the individual management, culture or primary goal of the organization, including: transformational leadership programmes and single operating models (used later in this chapter: case studies 1 and 2) – the premise for these frameworks being to assist leadership decision-making by explaining the relevance and contribution of tangible and intangible outcomes to a primary goal, building value chains across ambidextrous outcomes.

Conceptual balance mechanisms

We might characterize operational balance mechanisms as being designed as deliberate and explicit strategies, which means conceptual balance mechanisms might be considered as implicit strategies. These were found to be centred around subjective frameworks for leadership competencies, values and behaviours (see case study 3 later in this chapter). Similar to operational balance mechanisms, these frameworks set out to explain or legitimize ambidextrous behaviours by connecting them to a primary goal. Where they differed was in their tendency to be focused on leadership behaviours and mindsets rather than tasks, and being deliberately connected to the internal leadership appraisal system.

Various ambidextrous frameworks were found to be in place in all organizations participating in our research, reflecting strategies to keep pace with a dynamic and uncertain workplace, and the shifting attitudes, values, beliefs and philosophies of emerging generations of leadership talent. Participants

Figure 3: Balance mechanisms at a glance

Balance mechanism	Characteristically
Operational	Transformational leadership programme Single operating model
Conceptual	Leadership competencies framework Leadership behavioural model

described these strategies in general terms, designed to encourage change through innovation and creativity for high performance, by legitimizing unfamiliar, sometimes counter-intuitive, ways of thinking about leadership. How organizations pursue this new strategic leadership mindset is explored in the following three mini case studies.

Ambidextrous strategic frameworks: three case studies

CASE STUDY 1: A high-intensity public sector organization (Operational balance mechanism)

Context and ambidextrous challenge
Exploitative profile: A high-profile, public sector organization focused on reacting to unexpected external contingencies as part of an intensely dynamic context, subject to extreme levels of public scrutiny and accountability.
Explorative profile: A strategic directive from the CEO to overhaul current leadership thinking and behaviours, to reimagine today the shape and vison of the organization in five years' time.

The operational balance mechanism and hoped-for outcomes

To complete a transformational leadership programme that:

- Allows the organization to operate with less money, incorporating technological, communication and workforce changes.
- Transforms and modernizes the leadership culture (traditionally cynical and focused on here-and-now outcomes).
- Supports leaders to develop coaching behaviours for internal staff development and high performance.
- Allows leaders to make space to think about the future of the organization.

The ambidextrous framework

Table 2 Transformational leadership programme as part of an operational balance mechanism

Leadership category	Transformational leadership dimension	Transformational leadership coaching dimension	Transformational leadership coaching outcome	Transformational leadership organizational outcome
Leading for self	Understanding your leadership brand	Understanding the impact of your leadership on others	Leading operational change and adapting to new ideas	Efficiency savings: Retention Well-being Workspace
Leading for others	What your team needs from your leadership	Motivating and unlocking discretionary energy of teams	Developing new leadership behaviours (inc. coaching)	Performance: Results Promotions Recruitment Inclusivity
Leading for tomorrow	Developing your leadership mindset	Developing your leadership role	Envisioning your role in the organization of the future	Future relevance: Innovation Reputation Culture and values

---

Tips and exercises 8

Reflective exercise

After reading this case study, what are your key thoughts or reflections about the approach to evaluation?

What aspects of balance are you noticing?

How is the longer-term view being built into the design of the evaluation?

What tensions can you foresee in this setting or in your own practice?

What ideas, reflections or actions do you have related to your own practice?

A strategic A+

The ambidextrous framework is designed to explicitly link desired new and unfamiliar leadership thinking and behaviours, and accompanying coaching dimensions, to a strategy for a primary goal. Using three leadership categories, the framework creates a chain of explorative outcomes that connect to exploitative organizational targets. The framework is designed to facilitate a new style of leadership, focused on intangible outcomes and longer-term vision. The leader is encouraged to develop seemingly counter-intuitive (in the context of the primary goal) behaviours through the framework, which explains their relevance to a more readily understood exploitative target.

This transformational leadership programme, modelled as an ambidextrous framework, facilitates a change in the leadership mindset and provides a compelling case for leadership to be deliberate in thinking about the future, in an organization that is intuitively focused on the here and now, with an unwieldy (both in size and traditional attitudes) leadership cohort.

CASE STUDY 2: A third sector organization focused on a primary goal for purpose (Operational balance mechanism)

Context and ambidextrous challenge
Exploitative and explorative profile: A national youth poverty charity challenged to motivate a non-financially incentivized leadership cohort to deliver highly operational exploitative targets, under conditions of intense accountability, at odds with their personal motivations and the overarching explorative strategic vision of the organization: to end homelessness in a generation.
Ambidextrous perspective: This case study provides a distinct third sector perspective and presents an inverted ambidextrous challenge (focused on legitimizing exploitative, as opposed to explorative, targets). In contrast we found that the most likely scenario across private and public sector organizations is the justification of soft, intangible leadership behaviours and outcomes for a tangible monetary target.

The operational balance mechanism and hoped-for outcomes

To implement a single operating model that:

- Improves the experience of the 'customer' by creating a single line of sight for every job to a homeless person.
- Develops leadership mindsets to bust departmental silos.
- Explains the relevance of exploitative targets to the organizational purpose, subsequently enhancing leadership well-being and improving retention rates.

The ambidextrous model principle

The organization uses an operational balance mechanism in the form of a single operating model (SOM). The idea of the single operating model is to place the pivotal relationship between the key worker and the young person at the centre of the overall strategy. Therefore, the leadership hierarchy is inverted and senior directors are required to focus on the needs of frontline leaders: key workers, to create a direct route for every task, to a young person in poverty. In this way, the charity aims to build purpose into the leadership role, connecting to the bricks and mortar outcomes of the organization.

Tips and exercises 9

Reflective exercise — After reading this case study, what are your key thoughts or reflections about the approach to evaluation?

What aspects of balance did you notice that were different to the first case?

How else is the longer-term view being built into the design of the evaluation?

What additional tensions can you foresee in this setting or in your own practice?

What additional ideas, reflections or actions do you have related to your own practice?

A strategic A+

This single operating model uses ambidextrous dimensions to help build purpose into the leadership role. It is designed to break down traditional silo mentalities where departments have lost sight of the vision of the organization and developed a target-driven mentality focused on mainly exploitative outcomes. The knock-on effect of this meant leadership well-being was a problem with retention and there was a high rate of attrition. The model successfully legitimized hard short-term accountability targets by making sense of their contribution to a primary goal for purpose: to end youth poverty. In doing so, it managed the expectations of a leadership cohort that was not driven by financial self-interest, but considered purpose over profit as a career motivation.

CASE STUDY 3: A private sector global entertainment brand focused on a strategy to reimagine leadership (Conceptual balance mechanism)

Context and ambidextrous challenge
This is a private sector organization at a pivotal time, with a recently appointed CEO, moving from a 'cerebral to a disruptor senior leadership mindset'. This case study is an example of a conceptual balance mechanism in the form of a leadership competency framework. It also provides evidence of the influence of the CEO on the internal context of the organization, imprinting their unique cultural and philosophical values on the brand and forward strategy.

Exploitative and explorative profiles: The organization is focused on an adaptive strategy to respond to a rapidly evolving technological and talent context, delivered through its leadership cohort. It recognizes that, to be successful, it needs to change its leadership mindset to pursue high performance and profit through a balanced approach of short-term efficiency targets and a longer-term vision for future competitive relevance. Therefore, it requires a strategy to reimagine its leadership to promote management of financial risk in the day-to-day running of the business, and a creative fearlessness for future vision and innovation. As part of this restructure, the organizational leadership will be required to identify talent, accelerating succession to pivotal leadership roles, simultaneously dismantling the existing leadership hierarchy.

The conceptual balance mechanism and hoped for outcomes

To facilitate the CEO's ambition to reimagine leadership, through a leadership competency framework that:

- Produces savings and improves efficiency through streamlining leadership, implementing an ambitious spans and layers policy: reducing levels of leadership, removing managers managing managers.
- Focuses on communication and a culture of collective understanding.
- Responds to a dynamic marketplace (in both talent and technology) but anticipates bold visionary strategies to ensure future growth and high performance.
- Changes the leadership mindset from cerebral to market disruptor.

The ambidextrous framework

The organization has designed a leadership competency framework as a conceptual balance mechanism to spearhead its strategy. It has adopted five leadership categories, specifically focused on cognitive and behavioural criteria, all but one of which (problem solver) reflects the strategic emphasis on explorative leadership outcomes (conceptual balance mechanisms were found, throughout our research, to define emergent leadership expectations in explorative language, open to subjective interpretation, such as: trusted partner; good citizen; value added; servant-hearted and custodian. Therefore, relevant ambidextrous frameworks were also structural opportunities to explain these in terms of performance management, allowing the organization to provide wide-ranging definitions to language that was vulnerable to being perceived as merely rhetoric). In a similar way to operational balance mechanisms, the conceptual framework connects ambidextrous outcomes in exploitative and explorative chains; however, its principal function is as a leadership road map against which performance can be directly assessed. Therefore, unlike the operational framework, its impact on a primary goal is implicit.

It is worth highlighting the distinction the organization affords to its two leadership categories: organizational leader and people manager. Both categories have separate ambidextrous frameworks to clearly identify the leadership expectations for each group, providing an assurance of strategic alignment and boundaries for leadership responsibilities. We have included both versions here, overlaid onto a version of our own research framework (Table 1).

Table 3 Leadership competencies framework for organizational leaders

Competency: Organization leader	Balance – exploitation	Balance – exploration	Balancing act framework – coaching dimension	Implications for dimensions of evaluation
Trusted partner		Develops talent pools for succession	Managing multiple conflicting structures and systems	Emphasis on team management for pivotal roles
		Sought out for mentoring	Professional judgement	Well-being and engagement
		Invests in top talent	Social integration and relationship management	Fuller range of coaching outcomes

(Continued)

Table 3 (Continued)

Competency: Organization leader	Balance – exploitation	Balance – exploration	Balancing act framework – coaching dimension	Implications for dimensions of evaluation
		Champions organizational culture	Strategic alignment	Emphasis on culture of collective understanding
		Invites collaboration		
Effective communicator	Leads from the front, visible and accessible		Managing change	Emphasis on complex environment
		Explains vision and purpose for full commitment	Strategic alignment	Emphasis on culture of collective understanding
		Inspires others	Social integration and relationship management	Leadership perspectives
Strategic thinker	Modifies strategy according to business trends/ Designs an agile organization responsive to clients	Maps bold steps to grow organization Visionary	Managing change	Balanced complex environment with opportunity generation
Problem solver	Up to date on operating knowledge	Reassures others to use unproven problem-solving approaches	Managing change Strategic alignment	Balanced complex environment with opportunity generation
		Selects solutions for the greater good of the enterprise over parochial interest	Professional judgement	Emphasis on culture of collective understanding Well-being and engagement

(Continued)

Table 3 (Continued)

Competency: Organization leader	Balance – exploitation	Balance – exploration	Balancing act framework – coaching dimension	Implications for dimensions of evaluation
Change agent		Inspires others to constructively challenge the status quo taking well-calculated risks Creates a culture where mistakes are an opportunity to learn	Managing change Professional judgement Managing risk	Emphasis on complex environment Well-being and engagement Competitive relevance

Table 4 Leadership competencies framework for people managers

Competency: People manager	Balance – exploitation	Balance – exploration	Balancing act framework – coaching dimension	Implications for dimensions of evaluation
Trusted partner		Empowering others Sought out for mentoring	Social integration and relationship management	Emphasis on fuller range of coaching outcomes and leadership
		Identifies talent to build high performing teams	Managing multiple conflicting structures and systems	Emphasis on team management for pivotal roles
		Objective People Decisions	Professional judgement	Emphasis on well-being and engagement
Effective communicator	Delivers tough messages Negotiates Communicates tough messages		Managing risk Strategic alignment	Emphasis on budgetary justification to deliver culture of collective understanding

(Continued)

Table 4   (Continued)

Competency: People manager	Balance – exploitation	Balance – exploration	Balancing act framework – coaching dimension	Implications for dimensions of evaluation
Strategic thinker	Provides direction	Envisions and encourages future scenarios Encourages exploration of new opportunities	Managing risk	Balanced performance with competitive relevance
Problem solver	Judgements to prioritize client's needs based on business impact Solicits multiple points of view to develop viable solutions Refuses low value work		Managing change Professional judgement	Emphasis on complex environment Emphasis on RoI
Change agent		Sponsors creative ideas Generates innovation Promotes continuous improvement Focuses on value creation	Managing risk Managing change Professional judgement	Emphasis on competitive relevance Opportunity generation Employee engagement

---

Tips and exercises 10

Reflective
exercise

Across the three case studies, you have now read evaluation examples across private, public and voluntary sectors. What initial insights or lessons might you draw about the different settings, in terms of:

How strategic balance is achieved, where both operational and strategic issues are addressed:

The tensions faced when striving for ambidextrous evaluation:

What additional ideas, reflections or actions do you have related to your own practice?

A strategic A+

It is too early to assess the impact of this model as a strategic framework, due to its conceptual focus, its implicit nature and its emphasis on mainly explorative behaviours for long-term goals. However, it has supported a successful 'spans and layers' reorganization of the leadership structure and imprinted the incumbent CEO's values and philosophies on the brand. Despite the longer-term view of this strategy, its impact on talent, a key strategic focus for the organization, has been immediate, specifically in creating a sense of opportunity for top talent and addressing an environment characterized by rapid turnover. In doing so, it has achieved a key outcome for the reimagining of leadership: to successfully create space for dynamic new roles (by not replacing traditional management posts) and accelerate a new generation of talent into senior posts.

A third iteration of this framework covers 'All employees', ensuring the new leadership culture is able to extend its reach throughout the organization, encouraging employees to take responsibility for their professional and personal development as part of a new talent philosophy. Placing the framework across the whole organization also opens opportunities for lateral moves as a creative alternative to the more limited opportunities for upward promotions, and as another strategy to retain talent.

How ambidexterity exposed evaluation as a *Fail:* the practitioner default position for evaluation

End goals, culture and strategic disconnect: why evaluation is an inconvenience

In stark contrast to the wave of positive strategic opportunism released by ambidexterity, evaluation remained cast adrift from the new strategy mainstream. As we continue to shift our focus to examine *why?* (as opposed to *how?*) professionals fail to evaluate, we were interested in the attitudes of our research sample, and the responses given to the simple question:

> Given the ambidextrous systems you already have in place, why have you not extended these to include evaluation?

What we were looking for were the instinctive or default responses, to gauge the general appetite for evaluation. What we expected to find was a reversion to our three go-to justifications in defence of their record on evaluation: end goals, culture and strategic disconnect. And we were not disappointed. What we were encouraged by was that, as part of the general response, organizational stakeholders and coaches alike accepted that evaluation, for varying (mainly operational) motives, was a necessary function that either did not get done, or was done half-heartedly and ineffectively.

End goals

End goals was generally a reference to the evaluator's lack of ambition to assess explorative longer-term leadership outcomes. In terms of ambidexterity, this reflected the pressure of short-term foci, where expansive evaluation beyond day-to-day imperatives was considered a luxury, only afforded by high performance, assessed against exploitative targets. In other words, organizations found it difficult to find the space to consider the contribution of explorative outcomes as part of an ambidextrous chain, even if they were legitimized by being placed in the context of a primary goal, because they were consumed by the here and now. This senior director in a public sector organization explains:

> We have to make time to consider the impact of coaching on long-term goals and we are only really comfortable doing that when we have dealt with what's in front of us. The imperatives of our highly focused leadership environment inevitably get our evaluation attention.

Culture

In books such as these, *culture* gets a bad press. Open to subjective interpretations, an overused generalization, a lazy catch-all; but *culture*, like it or not, is a multifaceted concept that features as a primary influencer for evaluation throughout this book. The fascinating insights into the motivations and attitudes of professional evaluators, unlocked by examining the cultural context, means that *culture*, in one form or another, is one of our prime suspects in the case against evaluation.

Culture can be seen as either an instigator or an inhibitor of new ideas. In Chapter 1, for instance, we introduced the idea that the organizational culture helped shape and design new leadership and coaching outcomes, as part of a period of transition, characterized by creativity and experimentation. At the same time, it was clear that to extend this modernizing mood to include evaluation was a step too far. Organizations used their culture, in terms of brand (values, traditions, beliefs, etc.) or structure (size, market, age, etc.) to justify their position. This from the senior partner of a small, traditional private sector partnership:

> *We are small enough for equity partners to have a strong handle on how our leaders are developing ... if we were larger that wouldn't be the case and we'd probably have to think about a more formal system for evaluation.*

As we are beginning to learn, *culture* is a highly sensitive area, especially when evaluation is perceived as being synonymous with monetization. For now, we see it as a convenient excuse not to include evaluation in the newly adopted leadership strategies that preoccupy organizations today. What is certain is that we have not heard the last of *culture* as an influential force on evaluation.

Strategic disconnect

The most frequent example, used regularly throughout this book, of strategic disconnect, is the apparent gap between the operational (HR) function and the strategic (executive) function. However, another iteration is the disassociation between evaluation and the coaching process, as described here by the organizational stakeholder:

> *Yes, it's fair to say, amongst other things, this framework represents a possible evaluation tool – which we say we don't have. Although, we look at this framework to inform coaching outcomes, I suppose we just don't consider evaluation as part of the coaching package.*

More worryingly, strategic disconnect was often manifest as a complete lack of (unapologetic) awareness over the possible relevance of evaluation in terms of accountability or as a source of valuable strategic information. This executive articulates such complacency:

> *Coaching was just a facilitator of the results and outcomes we had decided upon – a means to an end. We only ever questioned the value for money of our leadership coaching programme when the bottom line was down.*

This lack of association supports our claim that, to many organizations, leadership coaching, despite its strategic prominence, remains an enigmatic investment, the impact of which investors are surprisingly content to casually assume.

What does the current mood for evaluation suggest? Exploring *why* professionals fail to grasp evaluation provides us with two valuable insights. Firstly, when presented with the wherewithal to expand existing ambidextrous logic to evaluation, practitioners use negative assumptions for justification as a smokescreen for complacency, disinterest or lack of strategic gumption. Secondly, external forces, albeit disruptive, are not the major source of evaluation barriers that conventional wisdom would have us believe, and the problems for evaluation actually might lie closer to home in the form of the unique organizational internal context (also known as its culture).

Summary of key points

Organizational ambidexterity is adopted as a context for research to replicate the current dynamic leadership environment. Ambidexterity was a familiar strategic concept and used by organizations as a vehicle for creative business solutions, connecting the new intangible expectations for leaders to tangible targets. Existing ambidextrous strategies were also found to negate traditional perspectives of evaluation problematics; however, these frameworks, despite opening up coaching dimensions, did not extend to evaluation of impact. An examination of practitioner attitudes starts to debunk what we thought we knew about barriers, revealing a level of complacency or lack of awareness towards evaluation that does not satisfactorily explain its failure to evolve with connected leadership strategies, and its treatment as a task or an inconvenience.

Chapter tool/template

Tool (for personal practice):

Quick-fire ambidexterity orientation audit

As a practitioner, it is useful to ascertain the orientations of your clients and how this aligns with your own preferences. This tool helps identify these orientations.

Use the template tool below to plot where you would estimate organizations, teams or groups.

	Tick here, if you are closer to the left	Tick here, if you are closer to the right	
Financial risk – pressing business imperatives with strong financial legitimacy			Cultural risk – long-term vision through innovation, creativity and capacity building with weak financial legitimacy
Respond – operate in a complex but known environment			Anticipate – operate in a complex but unknown environment
Scalability			Capacity building
Allocation of resources to areas of high impact			Allocation of resources to areas of future development
Recruitment and retention			Succession
Cost – training			Investment – coaching
Total			**Total**
Exploitative ambidextrous characteristics: short-term, known outcomes			**Explorative ambidextrous characteristics: long-term, unknown outcomes**

Quick-fire ambidexterity orientation audit

Use the dimensions below to plot where you would estimate ambidexterity orientation in a particular coaching evaluation. Use a separate sheet for each different evaluation.

This audit is for:

	Tick here, if you are closer to the left	Tick here, if you are closer to the right	
Financial risk – pressing business imperatives with strong financial legitimacy			Cultural risk – long-term vision through innovation, creativity and capacity building with weak financial legitimacy
Respond – operate in a complex but known environment			Anticipate – operate in a complex but unknown environment
Scalability			Capacity building
Allocation of resources to areas of high impact			Allocation of resources to areas of future development
Recruitment and retention			Succession
Cost – training			Investment – coaching
Total			**Total**
Exploitative ambidextrous characteristics: short-term, known outcomes			**Explorative ambidextrous characteristics: long-term, unknown outcomes**

What is the audit saying about the way this particular evaluation is designed?

The problem with evaluation lies in the organization's DNA

Chapter in brief

Having built the case over the last two chapters that it is perhaps the internal rather than the external context that significantly influences evaluation, this chapter begins an analysis of internal characteristics as the source of real-life evaluation tensions. Using a lens of ambidexterity, it redefines barriers as relatable working experiences that contribute to the paradoxical nature of evaluation. From these ideas, a refined understanding of the internal context emerges, replacing previously relied upon generalizations (end goals, culture and strategic disconnect) with practical interpretations: definitions, cultural sensitivities and the immiscible environment. This new knowledge supports our assertion that the internal context is unique to each organization and any future evaluation system will need to be tailor-made to the organization, with the flexibility to identify with and adapt to its unique DNA.

Introduction

This chapter argues that the failure to unlock evaluation is because, in seeking out solutions, theorists have been looking in the wrong place for answers to the wrong question. Conventional wisdom has persistently emphasized the external context, establishing intangible outcomes, disruptive external forces and a strategically aligned approach as the three main sources of evaluation frustrations. However, an examination of the real-life experience of evaluation practitioners reveals that external volatility and uncertainty is actually seen as a strategic opportunity, simultaneously negating perceived inhibitors and, rather than exacerbating evaluation, does in fact enable it. Therefore, if ambidexterity has disavowed external forces as the reason we struggle with evaluation, should we be looking for answers closer to home, focusing on the unique internal structures and systems within which today's leaders operate?

In this chapter, we move further away from the idea that evaluation fails because of contingencies outside the control of the evaluator, to explore the impact of the internal context, where the organization has, theoretically at least, absolute control. In doing so, we build the case for the unique organizational DNA: culture, philosophy, structures, values and goals, as the real source of evaluation barriers, manifest in real terms as a series of paradoxes. In redirecting our focus, we continue in our mission to address the question: why do organizations and coaches fail to connect to evaluation (and why should it matter)? Initially, we investigate how ambidexterity has impacted thinking around assumed barriers to evaluation. We then discuss three case studies, illustrating the influence of the internal context in real time, exploring organizational strategies and their relationships (or not) with evaluation, for insights and possible explanations. Finally, we refine our understanding of the internal context as a source of evaluation problematics, to better understand the components of a future evaluation design.

How ambidexterity has regenerated barriers as paradoxes

At the end of the last chapter we suggested that practitioners' reasoning for failing to engage with evaluation was a series of default responses, blaming internal malfunction caused by end goals, culture and strategic disconnect. Spotlighting internal machinations, over which the organization is the sole architect, implied that practitioners were finding excuses (consciously or subconsciously), albeit legitimate ones, to continue to treat evaluation as a task befitting mainly anecdotal data collection, limited to non-strategic outcomes, and considered of little value or importance.

Earlier in this book we discussed how using ambidexterity, to recreate the current leadership environment, has neutralized most of our assumptions about challenges to evaluation. Now, as we try to make sense of the persistent reluctance of practitioners to engage, we take a closer look at how preconceived barriers have evolved in real terms. Table 5 charts the evolution of broad-brush traditional barriers, filtered through a lens of ambidexterity. This process adds two new dimensions to our knowledge: how these actually manifest strategically in practice; and how they appear in the context of evaluation.

Table 5 The evolution of barriers from theory to practice

Barrier in theory	In practice (strategy)	In practice (evaluation)
Contingencies (external forces)	A springboard for strategy and a seedbed for innovative and creative solutions	Low strategic value placed on evaluation
Strategic alignment	Ambidextrous frameworks that link tangible targets and intangible goals in a chain of impact focused on a single primary goal	Evaluation contradicts organizational strategy
Intangibles	Ambidextrous strategies that isolate the contribution of counter-intuitive outcomes to a primary goal	Evaluation metrics conflict with valued outcomes

This table comprises the findings from our research (Jamieson, Wall and Moore 2020), the most striking element being the regeneration of conventional barriers to a series of three paradoxes. Our approach uses the central column as a filter for perceived barriers, providing an ambidextrous working context to develop new insights into practitioner challenges. What initially puzzled us was the lack of a logical connection between barriers and their corresponding practice manifestations. On reflection, we believed this to be further evidence of the gap between current theory and practice, and although an obviously recognizable connection would have been convenient, the fundamental revelation that barriers, when applied to a working context, actually appear as strategic paradoxes, was a eureka moment for our research.

Tips and exercises 11

Tip *Coaches can often find differences between what we say we do ('espoused') and what others can confirm we do ('in-use') – this applies to coaching evaluation as well as leadership behaviours. It is useful to find evidence (and disconfirming evidence) to triangulate our in-use leadership, coaching and evaluation practices.*

The first evaluation paradox

In the previous chapter, we provided illustrations of how organizations attach strategic value to a volatile external context, heralding a renaissance period for leadership characterized by new behaviours and thinking. Ambidextrous frameworks were used to facilitate transformational leadership, not only as part of a wider strategy for high performance, but also to mediate between leadership cohorts to encourage the adoption of emergent, often counter-intuitive, behaviours. Therefore, rather than exacerbate, contingencies surprised us by enabling organizations, providing a strategic springboard for creative solutions, simultaneously identifying expectations for leadership and coaching, and a clear line of sight for evaluation. This level of clarification also suggests an opportunity for a wider contribution from evaluation, as organizations seek valuable impact data to inform strategies to keep pace with the constantly moving target that is now leadership. However, despite the strategic emphasis placed on contingencies (the external context) and the potentially expansive offering from evaluation, the impact of coaching hardly registers on the executive agenda beyond superficial operational or accountability targets. This strategic lack of ambition extended to the findings from our research with coaches (Wall et al. 2017), where evaluation was mainly limited to tendentious outcomes of advocacy, marketing and business generation.

The second evaluation paradox

We also found that organizations were very deliberate in providing ambidextrous frameworks that delivered strategic alignment. Drawing on our research, respondents across all sectors reported a key challenge was to encourage leaders to accept the emerging coaching agenda for ambidexterity, specifically in terms of exploitative or explorative outcomes that were seemingly in conflict with the organization's primary goal. What was remarkable (as a subtext) about this part of our research was the tone adopted by our participating stakeholders, all of whom made strong verbal statements of intent with implications for leadership outcomes, performance management and coaching.

This response from the Director of People and Change at a highly accountable government organization was pretty typical:

> What we are trying to achieve strategically means we need our leaders to own that tension between long-term capacity building and delivering today. Despite the intense pressure they are under, they need to develop the agility and judgement to switch focus in the moment.

Statements of good intent, like this, were thematic throughout our research and, in fairness, organizations were found to have made attempts to support and encourage their leaders, designing practical explanations through the various operational and conceptual balance mechanisms described in Chapter 2. However, our data also suggested existing organizational operational structures were challenged to accommodate the emerging context in the same way that had seen strategic functions flourish, specifically in the context of evaluation. Here, we begin to get an inkling of the internal context as the dominant influential force for evaluation inhibitors. What we found was, ambidextrous frameworks designed to explain exploitative and explorative outcomes, making them relatable to leaders, were being undermined by internal organizational machinations: end goals; culture and strategic disconnect. This was exacerbated by performance management systems emphasizing a dominant primary goal or stakeholder, perpetuating a continued focus on short-term financial performance targets.

In short, ambidexterity was found to neutralize the problem of strategic alignment for evaluation, updating coaching dimensions and guiding leadership by providing a direct sightline to a primary goal. What we found surprising was how stakeholders continued to think about evaluation in a strategically unaligned way. As we scratched the surface of this second paradox we found how the influence of internal structures and systems corrupted or mismanaged ambidextrous strategies, resulting in an evaluation mindset at odds with a carefully crafted, much-vaunted overarching strategy. The fundamental contradiction between leadership strategy and evaluation focus exemplifies the inability of organizations to simultaneously adapt their internal operational context to the external strategic context.

The third paradox

Having dismissed contingencies as a non-barrier and reframed it as a strategic accelerator, and made the case for ambidexterity as having potentially annulled the challenge for strategically aligned evaluation, we finally turn our attention to intangibles. In Chapter 1, we discussed the need for inventive strategies that reimagined leadership expectations, and the subsequent exponential rise of coaching that accompanied them. The emphasis on intangible outcomes that characterized the new leadership approach was expected to add to the evaluation conundrum, exacerbating further the idiosyncratic nature of leadership coaching that has perplexed practitioners for time immemorial. However, despite increasing the complexity of evaluation by emphasizing the measurement of intangibles, ambidextrous frameworks effectively explained, and then isolated them, by placing them in the context of their contribution to a primary goal. Notwithstanding, evaluation thinking contradicted these frameworks, appearing as outdated, one-dimensional, focused on tangible short-term targets, or limited to traditional HR outcomes. In other words, organizations were found to have ignored the opportunity, presented to them by ambidexterity, to classify intangibles, resulting in their systematic failure to pursue evaluation of those goals they categorically stated as being most valuable.

In discrediting conventional thinking about evaluation barriers, we have subsequently reimagined these as working paradoxes. We believe this shift in thinking will help us in our quest to better understand the complicated relationship between leadership, leadership coaching and evaluation. Throughout this section, it has been implied that the internal context has conspired against the organizational strategy, especially if we accept that contingencies are no longer a barrier to evaluation, and strategic alignment and intangibles have been effectively negated by ambidextrous strategies. Building on these new insights, we now direct our gaze towards the inner workings, systems and structures of the organization in search of answers as to why they, and coaches, are failing to make the connection with evaluation. The following case studies examine various iterations of evaluation in practice, revealing how the unique internal context excludes evaluation from existing ambidextrous frameworks, and bringing to life evaluation paradoxes.

Tips and exercises 12

Reflective exercise | As you read through the paradoxes of coaching evaluation, what similarities and differences can you sense in your own coaching evaluation practice? What paradoxes have you noticed over your experience of coaching evaluation?

Case study 4: Evaluation paradox – evaluation contradicts organizational strategy

In this case, a private sector company is focused on a strategy of mergers and acquisitions to deliver a primary goal for profit for shareholders. The company has in place a number of ambidextrous strategies, balancing short-term profits with long-term opportunity generation, as articulated by the CEO:

> *You might say mergers and acquisitions is the ultimate ambidextrous strategy. On the one hand, we're providing short-term fixes to grow the value of the business, but on the other hand we are investing in the long term, and only then will our shareholders see dividends.*

The company has taken deliberate steps to create a collaborative executive (accommodating strategic and operational perspectives), including the HR director as a member of the executive board. However, despite best intentions, this appointment was ambiguous and clearly not fully integrated. The HR director described their position as a strategic facilitator, but with no commercial involvement:

> *I had two roles: the sole proprietor of our leadership development programme, and to implement the executive strategy. I was not involved in the commercial side of the business – that was not my job.*

Table 6 illustrates the resultant disconnect from the oil and water relationship between the operational and strategic wings of the organization.

Table 6   Lost in translation – the strategic disconnect between executive strategy and HR operational implementation

	Executive board (including HR)	
Executive strategy for performance		**HRD implementation strategy**
Mergers and acquisitions	→	Managing risk (legal)
Anticipate (opportunity generation)	→	Respond to complexity to manage change
Scalability (strategic as part of mergers and acquisitions business)	→	Scalability (operational to manage multiple conflicting structures and systems)
Allocation of resources to areas of high impact	→	Delivering a culture of collective understanding to manage strategic alignment
Capacity building	→	Recruitment and retention
RoI	→	Coaching efficacy

This table records the responses of the CEO and the HRD in the context of leadership outcomes to deliver an overarching strategy. Despite the presence of the HR function on the executive board, strategy appears to get lost in translation at the implementation stage due to the operational perspective contradicting the organizational vision. In turn, this restricted view sees the tail wagging the dog, limiting the scope of evaluation, confining it to operational targets, emphasizing the execution of strategy in a legal and responsible way, given precedence over the actual strategy itself.

Tips and exercises 13

Tip   *Conflictual relationships (oil and water) certainly have a role in the way coaching and coaching evaluation is done in practice. It is incredibly useful to be aware of this as you construct and then implement your evaluative work.*

Reflective   Do you get a sense of where the 'oil and water' relationships
exercise   generally exist in organizations – for example: Particular functional areas? Particular levels of management? Or different geographic parts of the business?

Thinking of your last coaching clients, reflect on any conflicts between groups and try to identify the source of those conflicts:

Example conflict 1 and a possible cause of it:

Example conflict 2 and a possible cause of it:

Example conflict 3 and a possible cause of it:

Case study 5: Evaluation paradox – low strategic value placed upon evaluation

Developing the model in case study 1, we examine the implications of an operational interpretation of an executive strategy by taking the evaluation process to the next stage. Figure 4 shows the evaluation process within the design of the operational stakeholder (the HRD), distorting the intended strategy, focusing on a set of barely recognizable and strategically limited leadership performance and coaching impact criteria. This example illustrates our second paradox, with an operational perspective placing a low strategic value on any future evaluation, limiting its scope to one-dimensional HR targets or short-term performance outcomes and coaching efficacy, in contrast to the high strategic expectations the executive has placed upon its leadership cohort and their coaches.

Figure 4: The implications of an operational interpretation of executive strategy and strategically limited evaluation criteria

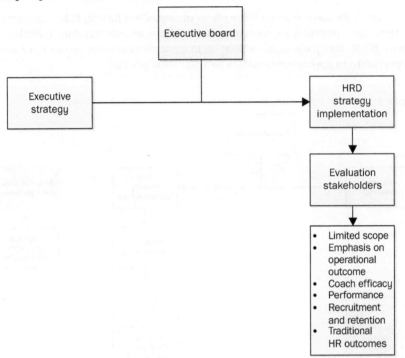

This is an interesting example of the implications of the disconnect between the operational and strategic arms of the organization; however, in this form, it is merely illustrative and really just reiterates what we already know, or at least, suspected. As part of our snowball research sample, this organization generously introduced us to their leadership coach provider. The subsequent data from this source produced fascinating insights into the tripartite relationship between the stakeholder, leader and coach in the context of evaluation. These produced a foundation stone upon which to build and formalize our thinking going forward: the immiscible environment for evaluation, where, despite their best efforts, strategic and operational viewpoints do not mix.

The headline findings from this subsequent set of interviews will go on to raise some uncomfortable questions for the organization; however, at this stage, the level of frustration felt by the coaching provider speaks volumes about the effective collaborative relationship as part of the coach contract, specifically where the HRD (the usual point of contact) is reluctant to have potentially difficult conversations with the executive:

> *Our coaches are in prime position to retrieve evaluation data to inform the client – for example, if you want to retain female leaders, adopt flexible working. This data tells us where the pressure points are, but our clients, HRDs, are generally timid about reporting to the board.*

In Figure 5 we have imagined the client organization having taken advantage of the coach provider's generous offer to share evaluation data (overlaid in grey). What our example of evaluation in a parallel universe shows is a missed opportunity to upgrade evaluation to a strategic priority.

Figure 5: A missed opportunity to upgrade evaluation to a strategic informant

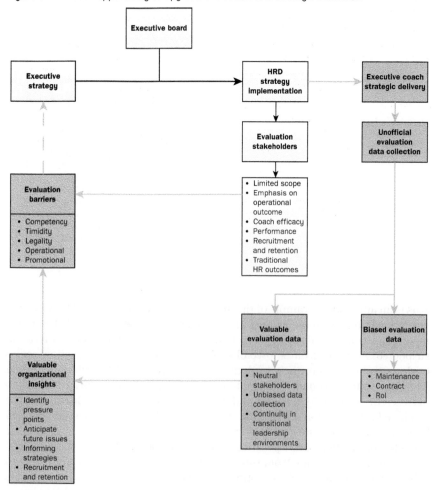

This case suggests the availability of valuable strategic data, which might usefully inform the organization's wider strategy through an evaluation conduit, is being deliberately blocked by the designated organizational stakeholder through a combination of internal miscommunication and a sense of proprietary rights from the HR directorate.

We would not presume to ask questions of the [sponsor] organization in this case; suffice to say, given the evident disconnect, there is scope to review its internal workings, specifically to narrow the gap between strategic and operational priorities, where current attempts have proved specious. It should also be pointed out, the evaluation approach of the coach organization was, in our experience, unusually diligent and stood alone among other coaching organizations we worked with, specifically in focusing on evaluation data as being strategically useful to the client organization, rather than self-serving promotion.

Tips and exercises 14

Tip | *Evaluation can sometimes carry difficult messages which contradict or highlight wider or more systemic issues – potentially more publicly than coaching itself. Rehearsal of your strategies to deliver these messages is critical.*

Reflective exercise | What are your experiences of delivering challenging messages which might contradict the shared view of the current situation? For example, that as a result of your work you have discovered leadership bullying is widespread, despite a view that the organization is respectful to all its employees?

What were the strategies you used?

How effective overall do you think your approach was?

Knowing what you know now, what would you do differently in your situation – and how might this inform how you deliver challenging evaluation messages now?

Case study 6: Evaluation paradox – evaluation metrics conflict with valued outcomes

To provide a balanced perspective, we have included a case that illustrates an entirely executive approach: a traditional partnership with no formal HR function, focused on a primary goal of financial performance for profit. This case places the unique organizational internal context centre stage, as a potential corruptor of evaluation, specifically where evaluation metrics conflict with valued outcomes.

In this example, the idiosyncrasies of governance ('We are a business built around traditional partnership principles: know, trust and respect'), and its relatively small size (around 500 employees), are used to legitimize discretionary judgements for evaluation made by equity partners with distinct attitudes to leadership development, emphasizing either exploitative or explorative outcomes inconsistently across the leadership group. Here, equity partners are the evaluation stakeholders, informally divided into either 'custodians' or 'brokers'. Custodians reportedly focus on the future health of the firm, emphasizing explorative outcomes for succession, capacity building, investment in leadership coaching, and future competitive relevance. Brokers, on the other hand, believe profit is king, and openly favour exploitative outcomes for short-term financial performance and efficiency saving.

This third case explains why evaluation metrics get corrupted and what is purported to be of value is not evaluated. In doing so, it also uncovers an additional layer of complexity, where the immiscible environment is not simply the gap between operational and strategic mindsets (in this instance there is no HR department), but the governance structure where, in theory, ownership is equitable across a group of partners, divided into two diametrically opposed camps. Using our own conceptual ambidextrous framework as a reference point, revealed the distinct attitude, not only to evaluation, but to the wider business philosophy, of the board of partners. Those self-styled custodians of the business were clearly motivated by: long-term goals (for future competitive relevance); talent development (for competitive differentiation); transformational leadership (culture of collective understanding); and nurturing leadership (for succession). In contrast, brokers were motivated by: profit (for financial performance); cost-cutting as a revenue stream (for efficiency saving); departmental performance (for internal budget as a source of profit); and management (for a distinct definition of leadership). Although both camps were focused on the same primary goal, Table 7 shows a strategic disconnect between the two sets of partners and a fundamentally different approach to achieving it. This, in turn, explains the resultant ambiguity over evaluation and contradictory, inconsistent metrics.

This case also proved that our generalized definitions of internally sourced evaluation inhibitors, although useful theoretical references, are practically limited, and will need to be refined and refocused to be adaptable to the unique design of an individual organization's evaluation needs. For instance, in this case, although end goals clearly focus on profit, there was discordance between partners over the definition of profit, as being either long term or short term.

Table 7   Strategic disconnect between partners sharing the same primary goal, corrupting evaluation metrics

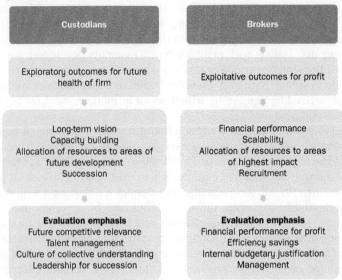

This divergence of opinion needs to be investigated as another, more complex layer of internal strategic disconnect, rendering our generalized definition as simplistic. As part of a knock-on effect, the different strategies to achieve end goals were also seen as a source of contradiction and tension, encouraged by leadership reward and recognition systems in place (as another dimension of its culture), designed to promote individual financial interests, but in a setting of collective ownership (where profit is shared equally).

Therefore, the internal context must be treated as a deeply complex landscape for evaluation, far more so than the impact of external contingencies, and it is these complexities that explain why practitioners might pass up the opportunity, afforded to them by ambidextrous strategies, to connect with evaluation. As we continue to develop thinking about what constitutes the internal context, necessarily, new, more specific identities need to evolve from our generalized categories to enhance our thinking about a future design. Accordingly, end goals, culture and strategic disconnect were redefined as: definitions, cultural sensitivities and the immiscible environment.

Refined characteristics of the internal context

Definitions

Initially we found organizations claiming end goals as reasons for not being able to pursue evaluation, generally referring to the pressure of delivering on short-term targets, and at the time, this catch-all term suited our purposes. End goals was a useful classification as we strove to understand the drivers for leadership, coaching and evaluation. However, as our investigations progressed, it soon became clear that this was too simplistic, too closely associated (and possibly confusingly so) with the idea of a primary goal. At the same time, as our discussions with evaluation professionals developed, we realized that one of the significant components of the internal context was that it was susceptible to subjectivity and, therefore, open to interpretation, suggesting it was characterized by ambiguity, which, as an influencer, went far beyond the scope of an end goal.

Throughout our research, we found that different definitions of goals, attitudes and timelines contributed to the unique internal context and, recognizing this, would be highly significant to our thinking on the design of a future model, finally dismissing the idea that evaluation can ever be an off-the-shelf product, or that one size fits all. Accordingly, any system we designed would need to have the flexibility to accept different definitions to accommodate, and be adaptable to, the individual organization, and this rendered our focus on end goals as one-dimensional and no longer effective. We have seen in all three case studies of how diverse definitions are not confined to sectors, but often sit within a single organization where stakeholders have varying interpretations of outcomes, attitudes, timelines and values. These different definitions (not solely end goals) characterize the turmoil of the internal context, which organizations accept as normal. In other words, ambiguity had evolved as a new primary focus and although end goals were included, the wider headline classification 'definitions' was felt to be more appropriate.

Cultural sensitivities

It would appear that we have just added the word 'sensitivities' to this category, but our continued research found this to be an apposite and meaningful addition that better described the practitioner's experience of the internal context in terms of evaluation. One of the major challenges for any organization seeking to be adaptive through leadership is the dismantling of existing structures, whether operational or strategic. This, however, is not simply a matter of busting silos or implementing transformational leadership programmes, but a far more deep-rooted change for behaviours and thinking that are often inherent, controversial or highly sensitive. For instance, it is often difficult for any organization to second guess what lies behind the insecurities of its leaders to create silos or adopt a proprietorial mentality. Equally, how does an organization switch to a safe environment for its leaders to challenge the conventional wisdom of a traditional way of doing or thinking? The culture of the organization is its unique selling point; however, it can also be its Achilles heel.

The immiscible environment

Earlier in this chapter we described the operational and strategic arms of the organization as an oil and water combination. Having delved more deeply into the internal context, it is clear that the concept of strategic disconnect is not confined to operational and executive functions. For example, in our third case study, no HR department was involved and the misalignment of evaluation targets came from the distinct attitudes of stakeholders. This idea was also extended to include some relationships between organizations and their coaches, where evaluation was seen as inappropriate (to the coach's values) or interference (from the organizational perspective: 'not your job'). This refined classification implies that the internal context is an unnatural collegiate environment where strategic disconnect is often a default position. However negative, this assumption grounds the evaluator, avoiding complacency and not underestimating the task that lies ahead, when setting about producing a resilient system.

Beginning to make the case for why evaluation matters

As a result of redressing the balance of research by focusing our attention on *why?* rather than *how?* organizations fail to evaluate, we are now beginning to see why it matters. And we should not forget that, by proving why evaluation counts, we are providing a potent incentive for stakeholders to take notice. Leadership is constantly evolving and it follows that organizations will continue to invest financially and strategically in their leaders' development to deliver adaptive strategies for high performance. Therefore, relevant evaluation data, capable of informing organizational strategists, is becoming highly sought after. In addition, we have seen how the internal context corrupts evaluation data, not to mention the overarching strategy, and now, more than ever, organizations seek a neutral arbiter to assess the progress of their leadership strategies, for which evaluation is ideally placed as a natural fulcrum for leadership, leadership outcomes and leadership coaching.

These three case studies illuminate the relationship between organizational ambidextrous strategies and evaluation, bringing to life the paradoxes emerging from previous assumptions about barriers. In doing so, they not only explain how practitioners struggle to connect with evaluation, but also provide insights as to why. The idea that we might simply tack evaluation onto existing ambidextrous structures is a convenient notion, and may go part way to satisfying practitioners focused solely on the question of how to evaluate. However, as these examples prove, evaluation is a more complex conundrum, not simply solved by cutting a Gordian knot, and progress will continue to be limited if evaluators persist in emphasizing practical functionality over intellectual dimensions (the *how?* over the *why?*). We need to solve both questions, so that evaluators are best served by a balanced approach: a workable and simultaneously strategically useful system.

Tips and exercises 15

Tip
Evaluation can sometimes be commissioned to give the impression of assurance and accountability, without making changes to leadership or strategy practices. This can lead to missed opportunities for longer-term impact, but there may well be sensitive or difficult conversations needed to realize strategic impact.

Reflective exercise
Coaching can sometimes miss optimal impact because of a disconnect between those commissioning the coaching and those in a position to make leadership or strategic impacts. What are your experiences of evaluation practice which did not lead to the level of change you expected? What do these experiences tell you about the success factors of enabling evaluation to make a difference?

Summary of key points

An examination of the internal context, as the main source of evaluation inhibitions, reveals a more complex proposition than previously imagined, by being vulnerable to subjective and discretionary interpretation due to cultural sensitivities. To break down our understanding of the internal context, in terms of the behaviours and mindset of the organization, we used ambidexterity to redefine barriers in a real-life setting. These emerged as three paradoxes, confirming our assumptions about the contradictory nature of evaluation made earlier in this book. A closer examination of these paradoxes refined our generalized understanding of those factors that drive the unique organizational context: definitions, cultural sensitivities and the immiscible environment. These new insights provide us with valuable knowledge for future design and how to evaluate, and, at the same time, begins to build the case for why it matters.

Chapter tool/template

Tool (for personal practice):

Stakeholder perspective analysis (personal reflection)

This template tool encourages proactive thinking about those who have an interest in the findings of a coaching evaluation and what this means for its design and implementation.

The tool asks you or a team to map out the specific views or perspectives of different stakeholders in that setting (a CEO, a CFO, a board, an HR manager, an employee, etc.). Then it explores which stakeholders are generally *supportive or lean towards* coaching evaluation and those which are generally *unsupportive or are against* evaluation.

This can be applied to a recent leadership coaching client, or at the design stage.

Stakeholder	Views/perspectives	Towards	Against

Stakeholder perspective analysis (team reflection)

The coaching I/we want to evaluate:

- In the first column below, list all of the stakeholders who will have an interest in the findings of the evaluation of different stakeholders (a CEO, a CFO, a board, an HR manager, an employee, etc.).
- In the second column, list why they would be interested.
- In the third column, for each stakeholder, write down their specific views or perspectives. Then try to identify whether they are generally *supportive and lean towards* coaching evaluation or generally *unsupportive and are against* evaluation.
- Once complete, reflect on what the analysis tells me/us about how we might need to approach the design or implementation of leadership coaching evaluation?

Stakeholder	Why they are interested	Views/perspectives	Towards	Against

4 A pivotal time for evaluation: influencers, insights and a question of will

Chapter in brief

It is a pivotal time for evaluation, as coaches and organizations move from the self-fulfilling prophecy that evaluation is limited, too difficult, or a combination of both, to the prospect of a workable system that is, simultaneously, strategically helpful. Ambidexterity has effectively disrupted the way we think about evaluation, removing theoretical assumptions about barriers and reframing them as real-life challenges (workplace paradoxes) emanating from the organizational DNA. An examination of these paradoxes produces new insights into the significant influencers of evaluation, from which four categories emerge: primary goals, evaluation status, multigenerational leadership pools and organizational context. Understanding how influencers engage and interact with evaluation is the first step along the way to designing a practical model. As part of this process, perceived problems are neutralized and strategic opportunities glimpsed, as evaluation begins to become, not only accessible, but a compelling prospect to the practitioner. Removing obstacles and providing evidence of strategic benefits makes evaluation difficult to ignore, and this raises questions for professionals, particularly, if they choose to continue to overlook evaluation.

Introduction

This chapter is a fulcrum for the book, as we move towards building our evaluation model, practically and intellectually, drilling deeper into the subject, turning assumptions into meaningful evaluation dimensions and questioning practitioner motivation. To achieve this shift, we need to move to a higher intensity of examination to interrogate assumptions, previously conveniently set aside. For instance, in the last chapter, we accepted the disconnectedness of conventional ideas about barriers and their evolved real-life manifestations as a series of paradoxes, as simply representative of the current confusion around evaluation. Similarly, we also casually accepted the default reasoning behind evaluation habits: definitions, cultural sensitivities and an immiscible environment, as an occupational hazard. The reader will appreciate that, to move the subject forward, we needed to work with convenient generalizations (even advanced ones). Furthermore, we did so knowing that we were mirroring practice complacency, but, that at some time, if we could put our finger on those factors that effectively influenced evaluation, we could use that knowledge to unlock the design of our future model.

We were also aware of a growing (in significance) subtext to the book. As we continued to develop the theory that evaluation inhibitors were not the result of external forces, but within the control of the organization, a fundamental question kept cropping up: do organizations and coaches actually have the will to evaluate? In designing a workable and strategically useful evaluation model, we felt we would be able to kill two birds with one stone: solving the mystery of evaluation and, in building a compelling case, testing the will of practitioners, where not to evaluate would require a wilful disregard of a potential source of valuable strategic data.

Introducing the four influencers of evaluation

To begin with, we set out to produce a seminal redefining of evaluation influencers. Drawing on reimagined evaluation barriers (as paradoxes) uncovered in the last chapter, we connected these to current evaluation practice and attitudes emerging from our research to arrive at a clear understanding of influential forces that we might eventually use as tools to unlock a future evaluation system. Table 8 shows how we unpacked the practice dimensions of the three paradoxes (formerly barriers) to produce four evaluation influencers.

As researchers, we are focused on converting new knowledge for practical gain, and our intention will be to restyle these influencers as evaluation tools, or levers, which we will later rely upon to design a future model. However, let us initially examine these for what they are: a synthesis of our research, and a relatable representation of the current practice environment for evaluation.

The four influencers of evaluation (in order of dominance)

Primary goals (and their evaluation loops)

Throughout this book, we have referred to primary goals when we wish to reference the organization's ultimate purpose for being. As our research has been across diverse sectors, primary goals have varied, generally ranging from profit (private sector), accountability (public sector) and purpose (third sector). In Chapter 3, we described how the primary goal acts as a fulcrum for different ambidextrous strategies, used by organizations as a focal point for building ambidextrous chains of exploitative and explorative outcomes, and making sense of counter-intuitive leadership targets. However, despite multiple

Table 8   Dimensions of evaluation paradoxes and emergent influencers

Paradox	Practice dimension	Emergent influencer
Low strategic status	Disinterested stakeholder Coach stakeholder Cultural fit	Organizational context
Contradicting strategy	Formal – as part of reward and recognition or performance management system Informal – lack of accountability or limited to Kirkpatrick levels 1 and 2	Evaluation status
Conflicting metrics	Financial performance: (profit) – focus on self-interest or exploitative targets (accountability) – focus on short-term imperatives	Primary goals
	Organizational performance: high levels of accountability Purposive performance: employee motivation and engagement Succession – flawed strategy Emerging leadership values and behaviours	Multigenerational leadership pools

interpretations, primary goals, in its role as an influencer, is characterized by its restrictive one-dimensionality.

Primary goals came through [our research] as the dominant driver for both leadership coaching strategies and evaluation approaches. As an influencer, we found that, as well as being a driver, primary goals also acted as a strait-jacket for evaluation by creating an evaluation-loop from which the organization was challenged to break out. We attributed the paradox – what is stated as being valuable is not evaluated – to various evaluation loops, where primary goals have the capacity to dominate evaluation metrics, overriding and contra-dicting the strategically creative outcomes espoused by stakeholders. Distinct evaluation loops were found across all organizational sectors, as illustrated in Table 9.

Tips and exercises 16

Tip   *Evaluation embeds feedback (or more accurately feed-forward) loops of information and action – the same as the classical plan-do-check-act of which there are many variants. This is key to how it generates strategic short- and long-term value.*

Table 9 Primary goals and their distinct evaluation loops

Sector	Primary goal	Evaluation loop
Private	Financial performance for profit	Compensation loop: reward and recognition systems assuming individual financial motivation for high performance
Public	Performance for operational accountability	Priority loop: short-term focus on exploitative high accountability targets to make space for evaluation of explorative goals
Third	Performance for purpose	Beholden loop: short-term focus despite long-term explorative primary goal dictated by stakeholder relationship

The influence of the primary goal in the private sector was shaped by the individual leader's personality, in terms of attitude and ambition, where primary goals for profit were systematically linked to financial self-interest. This created a difficult environment for evaluation, with resultant data vulnerable to bias, inconsistency and contradiction. In this way, monetary evaluation targets were locked into the system by internal reward packages as the assumed motivator for leadership performance that, in turn, only recognized narrow short-term financial outcomes, in a recurring evaluation loop, despite the stated long-term value priorities of stakeholders.

We found a different type of evaluation loop in the public sector, where primary goals were generally characterized as being high-accountability operational. In these organizations, primary goals were given priority and prohibited expansive evaluation beyond short-term imperatives. The evaluation of long-term goals was seen as a 'luxury' afforded by high performance assessed against (inevitably) a short-term exploitative target, designated by the primary goal.

Finally, in the third sector, where performance for purpose was deemed the explorative primary goal, we still found evaluation focus, turned inwards on more measurable exploitative targets such as financial accountability and management resources. Here, there was a sense of being beholden to a sponsor or donor and an inwardly focused, self-imposed accountability created an evaluation loop that restricted the evaluator to the targets or goals of the external stakeholder. The CEO explains:

> We have to evaluate because it is a cost and we are a charity. Somebody else is paying for our service – a local authority or a donor – and we have to be able to justify every penny we spend that doesn't directly relate to eradicating youth poverty.

Tips and exercises 17

Reflective exercise	Reflecting on a recent or current coaching evaluation, how does your experience resonate or connect with each of the loops in the table above?

To what extent are the loops determined by the private, public or third sector status of the organization? For example, have you experienced a compensation loop in the third sector?

What other loops have you seen in any private, public or third sector organization?

Evaluation status

We have talked about an immiscible environment for evaluation as one of the three generalized characteristics of the inhibiting influence of the internal context, but what does that mean in real terms for evaluation practitioners? Evaluation status generally refers to the oil and water components of the immiscible environment: operational and strategic, that comprise the non-harmonic organizational context for evaluation. Accordingly, we found that organizational evaluation stakeholders had either an operational (formal) or strategic (informal) mindset, which were generally incompatible. At the same time, the emergence of new leadership thinking, and the coaching that accompanies it, are challenging organizations to move away from the traditional HR management mindset, blamed for restricting evaluation data, to narrow the gap between formal and informal status for a more balanced approach. However, evidence suggests, this is an evolutionary rather than a revolutionary process, and will continue to perplex evaluators for some time to come.

Our research found that formal status was closely, almost rigidly, aligned to a primary goal, dominant stakeholder or operational balance mechanism for transformational leadership, inextricably linked to internal leadership appraisal systems. In all cases where evaluation status was formal, the evaluation approach was operational, as either an HR task, or through various leadership assessment systems, including reward and recognition, meaning that overall strategic alignment was compromised. In terms of our paradoxes, here evaluation, contradicted organizational strategy. In these instances, strategic outcomes were either interpreted as operational, or emphasized the exploitative targets in the ambidextrous chain despite deliberate attempts by the organization to evidence their value or legitimacy.

In one example, where agreed explorative coaching dimensions focused on creative and innovative leadership to deliver strategies for competitive differentiation for financial high performance, the participating CEO reported coaching impact was actually evaluated on leadership responsiveness (to short-term targets), recruitment and retention, and management of financial risk. It would be unfair to say the tone of this response was dismissive; however, there was a strong sense of *fait accompli*.

> *Our evaluation structure, such as it is, doesn't have the range to go beyond targets that are not easily financially recognizable.*

The relationship between formal status and performance management drives the skewed logic that sees organizations focusing on strategically unaligned criteria. One knock-on effect of this approach is that investment in leadership coaching is being undermined, with espoused coaching outcomes underused by leaders because, in the final judgement, they are being assessed and rewarded on straightforward financial performance against [strategically] unevolved targets.

Whereas formal evaluation status was recognized by practitioners variously, as an obligation or a task, those organizations applying informal status to evaluation were defensive about what they acknowledged as a more haphazard approach. In these organizations, participants were quick to justify an informal process reverting to default positions for definitions, cultural sensitivities and an immiscible environment. We found that informal status was accompanied by a lack of accountability, unsurprising for an unstructured system, where senior managers were assumed to pick up the responsibility to evaluate, almost incidentally. With reference to Kirkpatrick's seminal four levels evaluation model (see below: A word on Kirkpatrick), we noticed that evaluation data collection was confined to anecdotal evidence, specifically: the experience of the coachee and that of colleagues and peers as part of a 360-degree appraisal process.

Tips and exercises 18

Reflective exercise | In your own context, for example as an internal or external coach, what would you say is the *primary* goal driving your coaching? If you can't identify a single driving goal, how might this tension be presenting itself in your evaluation?

A word on Kirkpatrick

No book on evaluation is complete without reference to Kirkpatrick, who we credit with inventing modern-day evaluation for the effectiveness of executive development – in 1959! Although Kirkpatrick's four-level model (assessment at reaction, learning, behaviour and outcome levels) was formulated well over half a century ago, it endures, at both practitioner level (in 2013, the CIPD reported more than half of their survey sample used a variation of Kirkpatrick's four-level model, the majority of whom measured no further than the initial reaction stage), and at research level, as a foundation for future design (notably, Phillips' additional level: RoI, introduced in 1994), despite criticism that it is designed around outdated external and internal contexts.

The question is why Kirkpatrick, far from being irrelevant as a model for a very different time, continues to influence evaluation thinking? This is in part due to its simplicity, specifically, bridging the gap between theory and practice. There has been a whole raft of complex and confusing models and formulae since Kirkpatrick, producing a surfeit of irrelevant uninspiring data. Indeed, one of the key thrusts of this book is the argument that stakeholders are put off by evaluation at a time of intensifying accountability, due to the complexity of new theories aimed at targets of little interest. In other words, Kirkpatrick has endured because evaluation professionals have not been well served by evaluation theorists – nothing better has come along.

Another theme of this book goes some way to explaining Kirkpatrick's longevity: our preoccupation with how to evaluate rather than why we should evaluate. Kirkpatrick taught us how to evaluate, but not why we should. The muddled thinking around how to evaluate provides a convenient excuse for practitioners to either disregard evaluation as a too complex task, or go through the motions using anecdotal evidence, generally confined to Kirkpatrick's levels 1 and 2.

Tips and exercises 19

Tip *The most common practice of evaluation is rooted in models from the 1950s – despite organizations and contexts radically changing since then.*

As we examine the idea of evaluation status as an influencer, we should state that our preliminary vision of a compelling evaluation model does not necessarily require a shift from one extreme to another, rather, a subtle collaboration of the two, which in essence will provide an accessible framework for leadership creativity – whereas, to continue the binary distinction between formal and informal approaches, leaves evaluation open to either limited operational data, or unsupervised subjective judgements, neither of which are strategically helpful.

Multigenerational leadership pools

Multigenerational leadership pools represent the complexity of a pivotal time in workplace demographics, and is a three-dimensional influencer of evaluation. Using our conceptual ambidextrous framework as a reference, three generational pressure points emerged: succession, promotion, recruitment and retention (see Table 10).

In the form of various internal leadership hierarchies, these were found to contribute to the paradox for conflicting evaluation metrics, where senior strategists made bold statements of good intent around succession that were unmatched in terms of evaluation priorities. For most, succession was an agreed key responsibility for leaders, not only to grow the organization, but as a wider retention strategy. Here, the CEO of a private sector organization explains:

> We must encourage the generation below to see there is a career path for them to follow, making sure we make room for them to be able to grow the business in the long term.

However, without an evaluation mechanism in place, leaders are not being held to account sufficiently and have become the architects of their own Escher-like staircase: aiming for effective succession; impeded by a perceived vacuum of suitable talent beneath the incumbent executive; as a direct result of their contribution to deeply flawed succession planning. The implications of this dichotomy potentially undermine the wider strategy and cast doubt (to anyone outside the leadership cohort) over the commitment of the organization to hold to its espoused values and beliefs. On the other hand, the strategic usefulness of an evaluation system would not only act in a supervisory capacity for leadership, but produce insights into the leadership mindset through strategic data which could be applied to future succession planning.

Simplistically, it could be argued, this is a perfect storm moment for multiple generations in the workplace, and an awkward period of transition between groups retiring, succeeding and developing. However, participants in our research suggested a more complex, psychological conundrum, each pointing a finger at the other's character as responsible for a challenging environment for succession.

At one level, respondents were brutally frank about an incumbent leadership group that found it difficult to hand over to the next generation, whatever they might say in public. This inevitably had implications for evaluation and the veracity of resultant data, as described by the senior partner of a private sector firm:

> As a generation we are not good at facilitating succession. Evaluation data are vulnerable to distortion. A poor response [in terms of promotion criteria] was not necessarily down to the programme but often the flawed character of leaders who find it difficult to promote.

To place this in context, this comment referred to evaluation of coaching impact assessed by targets for promotion. The presumed deviousness of leadership character meant that resultant data was liable to being corrupted by the self-interest of current leaders. However, it could be argued, this is an unfair defamation of leadership character and, in practical terms, is the result of an internal structure that does not encourage succession by providing a parachute strategy for retiring executives. Either way we would claim that an evaluation strategy would provide valuable insights into both possibilities.

Different definitions of advancement were also exacerbating succession strategies. Here, some participants reported cultural divergence between generations over leadership pathways, specifically over promotion, values alignment and career development. These issues were magnified by limited promotion opportunities due to organizational structures and reluctant leadership retirees, and the resultant requirement to be creative in advancing, and therefore recruiting and retaining, leadership talent.

Tips and exercises 20

Tip *We are thinking more and more about opportunity and (dis)advantage in terms of the intersectionality of characteristics of age, gender, ethnicity, (dis)ability, sexual orientation, and so on. Age can often be tied up with gender and ethnicity creating multiple levels of opportunity and (dis)advantage, and have dramatically different impacts in different organizations, jobs/roles, occupations and sectors – it is important to be aware of such situations.*

Simultaneously, generational differences highlight the unique expectations placed on leadership coaching, to span all three generations of leaders, adding yet more layers of complexity to evaluation, including: timeline expectations, shifting values and philosophies, and potentially tendentious, subjective judgements from evaluation stakeholders. Table 10 illustrates the possible evaluation focus (leadership outcomes) under the influence of multigenerational leadership pools.

Table 10 Distinct leadership and coaching outcomes across multigenerational pools, with specific targets for evaluation

Generational perspective	Evaluation pressure point	Leadership outcomes
Incumbent leader	Succession	Identify and develop successor Smooth transition with effective handover period Recognition for long-term performance of successor
Succeeding leader	Promotion	Ability to 'hit ground running' Distinct leadership projects Wider contribution
Leadership talent pool	Recruitment and retention	Taking on early leadership roles Building reputation Developing strategic mindset

This framework provides an opportunity for the organization, through evaluation, to be specific about leadership expectations, accommodating distinct leadership coaching targets and timelines. In doing so, it provides us with an early glimpse of the potential practical impact of applying influencers as a tool for evaluation (clearly identifying with targets), as well as the strategic potential of evaluation as a source of valuable data.

As an influencer, multigenerational leadership pools, if used correctly, disambiguate the concept of different leadership cohorts for the organization and the coach. However, for the organization or coach who treats leadership as generic, this example exposes a simplistic approach for an extremely complex area.

Tips and exercises 21

Reflective exercise

To what extent is multigenerational leadership a strength or development area in your context (e.g. your organization, or a client you are working with at the moment)?

In your organization and sector, what have you noted about how age, gender or ethnicity are linked to opportunity and (dis)advantage? Industry reports can be very helpful in sensitizing yourself to particular issues.

Organizational context

Let us first address any potential confusion between the *internal context* and the *organizational context*. We use the *internal context* (definitions, cultural sensitivities and the immiscible environment) and the *external context* (political, demographic, economic, global, etc.) to explain the two major influential forces that can interact with the organization. The *organizational context*, on the other hand, is a subsection of the *internal context,* and refers to those, intangible, less easily explained factors that influence attitudes and approaches, specifically to evaluation. Culture is an interesting word because it is so open to interpretation, and as we look to break down the more generalized influential characteristics of the internal context, *cultural sensitivities* is replaced by *organizational context* as a practical tool for application.

When we discuss the *organizational context*, we are focusing on the values, ethics, philosophies, governance, personality and goals – in other words, the unique DNA – of the organization. The *organizational context* encompasses the intangible dimensions of our four influencers, specifically in terms of data consistency; competency of data collection and dissemination; and the landscape for evaluation as a strategic entity. Our research found a vast range of unique perspectives and evaluation impact points in this category, including the influence of the CEO, cynical attitudes towards a coaching environment and internal governance. It was also found to be a convenient catch-all excuse, or justification, for evaluation limitations, informal approaches, and the casual dismissal of evaluation as a task with low strategic status.

Whereas our other categories have an explicit influence on evaluation, *organizational context* impacts implicitly. We found this influencer in play with all three of our evaluation paradoxes, and considered its classification as an overarching influencer, such was its scope. However, we judged, that would be to try to conveniently simplify the most complicated and enigmatic component of the internal context, and left it as one of our four influencers, albeit with its possible role as a wildcard.

How influencers impacted the coach and raised questions about the coach–client relationship

Our previous research, focused on leadership coaches (Wall et al. 2017), proved invaluable in providing an all-round perspective of attitudes towards evaluation, completing the picture by allowing us to focus on the coach evaluator. Developing new knowledge about those factors that effectively influence evaluation, we were able to gain insights into the implications for leadership coaches. At the same time, these additional dimensions of knowledge framed a number of new questions about attitudes to evaluation, and the coach–client relationship, as a key subtext for this book.

At face value, influencers had significant implications for the coaching approach (Table 11), with the coach becoming immersed in the unique tensions of the client organization's internal context.

Table 11 Evaluation influencers – implications for the coach evaluator

Evaluation influencer	Implication for coach evaluator
Primary goal	• Organizational accountability and pressure on short-term targets over espoused coaching outcomes • Emerging intangible goals
Evaluation status	• Strategic disconnect with HR • Disengaged executive • Questions over responsibility • Schrödinger's cat complex
Multigenerational leadership pools	• Elevated status of C-suite coaches
Organizational context	• Conflation of evaluation with RoI • International context • Coaching practice

What we were interested to explore was how our four influencers were perceived by the evaluator coach and what this might mean for, not only the evaluation process, but the structure of the coach contract:

Primary goal – a coach evaluator perspective

Our research for the EMCC (Wall et al. 2017) found primary goals dominated the coach's attitude to evaluation, which, on the whole, was mutually (organization and coach) transactionally motivated. Initially, strategically unambitious organizations were limited to looking for monetary proof to justify their investment and, at the same time, coaches were keen to provide advocacy for their work to protect future contracts. Inevitably, this focused the coach away from the agreed outcomes they were being paid to deliver, to bottom-line accountability targets that they were not. In this way, the coach bore the brunt of the evaluation paradox, faced with a balancing act to accommodate a new set of leadership outcomes with financial accountability. This coach explains:

> My client's primary goal is purely financial performance. At the same time, I'm being tasked to deliver coaching around behaviours that are difficult to monetize. The challenge for coaches now is measuring the magic of coaching, and connecting it to the bottom line.

Evaluation status – a coach evaluator perspective

Evaluation status reflected the formal and informal approaches of organizations and exposed the often fractured or non-collaborative relationship between the coach and the client, at both operational and strategic levels. The operational disconnect, discussed generally in this book from an organizational perspective, was mirrored by this coach, where there was a sense of evaluation as a box-ticking exercise with scant evidence of strategic alignment:

> I've never worked with HR where they have even attempted to align coaching to a wider strategy. As coaches, we are engaged with very little evidence or reference to KPIs, when our point of contact with the client is via the HR director.

Alternatively, at the executive (strategic) end of the evaluation status spectrum, difficulties in securing senior management support for evaluation was thematic, giving credence to our suspicion that the will to evaluate might well be a significant and insidious barrier to evaluation:

> My main problem is to persuade senior management that we need to measure what we are doing. Unfortunately, we generally find a lack of buy-in from the CEOs we work for, and there is very little sign of commitment to follow up coaching programmes.

Evaluation: whose responsibility is it anyway?

Evaluation status also raised questions between the organization and the coach over responsibility, which included absolute abdication, proprietary right, and ethical considerations. In some cases, we found the coach dismissive of evaluation, which, it could be argued, diminished their role:

> *I do not think it's my role to evaluate – it's the client's responsibility; after all, it's their achievement, I am merely the facilitator.*

In other instances, organizational stakeholders were indignant at the coach's affrontery for suggesting evaluation as part of an integrated offering, considering it: 'not your place'. Lastly, concerns over client confidentiality as part of the coach contract appeared to close the door on evaluation, reflecting the coach's contribution as an external consultant rather than an internal confidant. Mixed messages for responsibility made this a grey area, with the likelihood that evaluation would fall between the cracks and be completely overlooked.

Finally, we were surprised (and perplexed) by the Schrödinger's cat complex we uncovered in our research, where it was reported that the complexity of making strategic judgements from a non-strategic mindset inhibited the evaluation process (underpinning our earlier assertion that formal status was characterized by the timidity of operational directors reporting to the executive) despite an agreed strategy, the level of investment and accountability trends:

> *When times are uncertain, some stakeholders actually avoid evaluations. They do not want to be accountable for investments they do not necessarily understand.*

This phenomenon suggested some organizations were happiest not knowing the impact of their investment, undermining their entire leadership development strategy as specious, asking questions, not only of the executive board, but any coach willing to work for an organization casually going through the motions.

Multigenerational leadership pools – a coach evaluator perspective

In our EMCC report, the concept of multigenerational leadership pools was underresearched, with most participants focused on C-suite leadership. However, when we applied this influencer to our coach data, one fascinating insight emerged from the narrow focus on the incumbent leadership cohort: the inflated status coaches gave themselves when talking about attitudes to evaluation. The tone of these types of response arguably reflects a degree of conceit or self-importance in the act of dismissing the idea, or responsibility for evaluation, as well as a limiting attitude towards continuing professional development:

> *I am very secure about the value I deliver as a coach. At the level I coach [CEOs] my clients are aware of their own outcomes and the effectiveness of my coaching – they do not require further evidence.*

Organizational context – a coach evaluator perspective

Organizational context continues to act (from a coach perspective) as a conduit for culture and idiosyncrasies, most interestingly from country to country (as opposed to organization to organization). Our research (ranging across European and American coaching practices) revealed different countries were at different stages of development in their experiences of coaching and evaluation:

> *Coaching, let alone evaluation, in this country is still 'science fiction'; you have to consider us as a 'baby' compared to the USA or UK.* Eastern European coach

Responses also reflected the indigenous leadership character and attitude to coaching, which was not always seen as developmental but, in some cases, shrouded in secrecy, as remedial and a sign of leadership weakness. Participants from less advanced countries also talked about an absence of any evaluation culture as part of a fractured relationship with the client, arguably reflecting strategic naivety:

> *Nobody wants to talk about evaluation, outcomes, RoI ... there is a lack of interest; sometimes my clients don't even want to meet me.* Central European coach

The implications from this final response provoke wider questions about the organizational coaching investment, and the coach's primary motivation, where neither party appear to be engaged in a collaborative contract. In these cases it can be argued that both parties' drivers are questionable, the upshot being that coaching is seen as a business or a marketing tool to attract talent, rather than a development strategy.

Lastly, similarly with the organizations with whom they worked, coaches often conflated evaluation with RoI. Here we found two schools of thought: coaches that acknowledged evaluation for RoI as necessary or desired, but limited and lacking credibility both financially and culturally:

> *I question the credibility of RoI when figures such as 675% are quoted. Also, organizations that are only focused on money – are their evaluation processes really fit for future purpose, with leadership targets changing so fast?*

And coaches who distanced themselves from evaluation for RoI as offending their cultural sensibilities, often in tones that variously projected lofty principles:

> *Evaluation [RoI] does not complement my style of coaching and is inappropriate. For my clients, it's more about how they are feeling – how would you monetize that? If I'm bound by a client to provide monetary evidence of impact, I would walk away.*

Questions of resolve

We have seen that an exploration of evaluation influencers has raised a number of, sometimes provocative, questions, suggesting evaluation is unattainable until those organizations have addressed wider conceptual issues around their drivers to commission leadership coaching programmes, and the quality of those programmes. More generally, one fundamental question continues to overshadow our work: a question of resolve. Earlier, we argued the case that this is a pivotal time for evaluation, but what do we mean by that?

Leadership and leadership coaching have experienced an accelerated period of development since the GFC in 2008 and evidence suggests that, for whatever reason, it has not really mattered to professionals that evaluation has stood still, focused on outdated irrelevant targets, despite high financial and intellectual investment. In turn, ambidexterity has shown a way to practically evaluate by negating assumed challenges, and signposting why evaluation might be strategically useful. Given the fact that ambidexterity has opened the way for a workable, strategically helpful system, the question that looms large is: where there is a way, is there a will?

The track record for evaluation is not promising. We found throughout our research that the attitudes and experiences of practitioners reflected the challenges and thinking posited three decades ago (evinced by the continued reliance on Kirkpatrick's four-level model designed in 1959). We challenge practitioners to break this process of fossilization at a time when data to inform ever more creative and innovative strategies is at a premium and new insights into influencers, suggesting evaluation and the internal context are inextricably linked, underpin the claim that practical evaluation is within our grasp and resultant data can be strategically valuable. Therefore, this is a pivotal time for evaluation and the compelling case we are building is set to test organizations and coaches, to find out whether a continued lack of progress is the result of a fractious period of transition, or whether practitioners are wilfully disregarding the opportunities presented to them to elicit valuable strategic data for their organization. Now, all we have to do, is design our evaluation system.

Summary of key points

At a pivotal time for evaluation, practitioners must make a choice whether or not to adopt new ideas that are claimed to be highly beneficial, both operationally and strategically. Among these new ideas, paradoxes (reimagined barriers) are examined through the experiences of practitioners to produce four key evaluation influencers: primary goals; evaluation status; multigenerational leadership pools; organizational context. The impact of these influencers is subtly distinct between organizational and coach evaluators, but asks similarly provocative questions of both attitudes and working practices. Having provided a new layer of understanding about how evaluation works, these four influencers will eventually be put to work to unlock a compelling evaluation system, recognizing the flexibility to serve the unique internal context, for practitioners to choose (or not).

Chapter tool/template

Tool (for personal and team practice):

Evaluation loop-breaker (personal and team reflection)

This tool encourages proactive thinking about what breaks the loop between evaluation findings and improvement action – and what this means for its design and implementation.

On a feedback diagram (example is given in Figure 6), a numbered 'X' is placed on the feedback loop and a few words are noted as to what is stopping the findings from evaluation from changing practice. After this, and for each 'X', ideas to mitigate each barrier are generated.

This can be applied to an organizational client, to consider the evaluation findings of a recent leadership coaching client, or the design stage to help think through the design and implementation stages.

Figure 6: Evaluation loop-breaker (personal and team reflection)

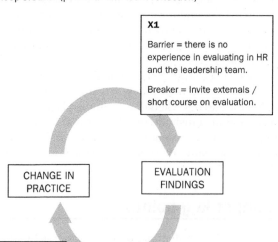

X1

Barrier = there is no experience in evaluating in HR and the leadership team.

Breaker = Invite externals / short course on evaluation.

CHANGE IN PRACTICE

EVALUATION FINDINGS

X2

Barrier = evaluators (HR) are a different group to those being evaluated (team leads in engineering).

Breaker = Invite team leads to get involved in evaluation?

5 How to evaluate: Part 1 – Using evaluation levers and ambidextrous frameworks

Chapter in brief

In this chapter, we convert new knowledge into design principles as we begin the process of building our evaluation model. Using an example organization as a demonstrable context, we describe the process through the three phases of evaluation: setting a context, designing a system and providing a strategic destination for data. To do so, we convert our four key influencers into levers, and apply these to the unique internal context to produce a clear understanding of inhibitors, from which six new dimensions for barriers emerge (as evaluation challenges), to help us arrive at the components of a workable system. We then use ambidexterity to shine a light on existing, strategic organizational machinations, to pinpoint relevant strategic targets for resultant evaluation data.

Introduction

Building on the foundations of the last chapter, we begin to convert the theory we have generated into practice, to design and build our workable, strategic evaluation model. To illustrate this process, we use a private sector organization focused on a primary goal for profit, via a leadership strategy for talent management for high financial performance, as a context for demonstration. We track the evolution of our evaluation model through three stages: context, design and strategic dissemination. Using new knowledge about influencers as tools, or levers, we map out the unique organizational landscape for evaluation, to elicit a real-life understanding of barriers, now reimagined as challenges, to develop an inventory of needs as the basis for a practical framework. Finally, we apply our second tool, ambidexterity, to illuminate the strategic potential of resultant data.

Tips and exercises 22

Tip

Ambidexterity might be usefully thought of as the creative integration of structure (to direct towards known outcomes) and freedom (to explore towards new insights). We often refer to a 'strawperson', 'working model' or 'working draft' in coaching, coach training, and in business practices. We advocate you do the same for evaluation – and use your reflections in this chapter to help build and craft your own working models as you develop your awareness of situations. We do emphasize that this is a working model, so is sensitive to context and new insight as you develop.

Reflective exercise

How would you describe your current process for leadership coaching evaluation? You might use the space below to write down your steps as a numbered list, a set of questions, or you might prefer to draw them as interconnecting areas of awareness – whichever best represents your awareness and knowledge at the moment. You might integrate new insights from previous training or from reading this book. This will help integrate and consolidate your key top-of-mind awareness right now.

Evaluation stage 1 – Setting the context

Applying influencers as levers for a better understanding of evaluation inhibitions

Firstly, let us start by reinventing the key influencers developed in Chapter 4, as evaluation tools, or levers, and put these to work, connecting the generalized problem areas, thematic throughout our research (data usage, dissemination, timelines and competency), to the current leadership context, replicated by ambidexterity. Applying evaluation levers unlocked the dimensions of these problem areas, allowing us to interpret them across the conceptual framework as ambidextrous leadership (and coaching) foci and, ultimately, future targets for evaluation. The idea of connecting levers to a real-world leadership environment is to help us develop a more sophisticated understanding of the organization's evaluation inhibitors, and the landscape (challenging or otherwise) within which our evaluation model will be designed. In Table 12, through the application of levers, we can convert the default responses of participants into multidimensional definitions, to explain these in practical terms, relatable to leaders and insightful to coaches. Encompassing ambidextrous leadership coaching dimensions in this process, also allowed us to invite the coach to begin to collaborate with the organization, not yet in terms of evaluation, but more generally as part of a diagnostic tool for leadership outcomes. This foundational understanding provides us with the platform for our workable evaluation system.

Table 12   Applying evaluation levers to problem areas to produce practice dimensions and insights into the coaching task

Problem area	Evaluation lever	Emergent dimensions of problem	Ambidextrous leadership and coaching focus
Data usage	Primary goal	Reward and recognition system	Budgetary justification versus culture of collective understanding
		Performance management system	**Performance versus future competitive relevance**
		Advocacy (coach)	Coaching efficacy versus full range of outcomes
Dissemination	Evaluation status	**Operational or strategic**	**Complex environment versus opportunity**
		Formal or informal	**generation**
		Relevant data	Efficiency savings versus talent
		Multiple stakeholders	management for high-impact roles

(Continued)

Table 12 (Continued)

Problem area	Evaluation lever	Emergent dimensions of problem	Ambidextrous leadership and coaching focus
Timelines	Multigenerational leadership pools	**Leadership transition** Succession **Coaching impact timelines** Retention of high potentials	**Management versus leadership**
Competency	Organizational context	**Cultural diversity** Subjectivity **Bias** Inconsistency	Budgetary justification versus culture of collective understanding

Secondly, we developed a version of this table (Table 13), synthesizing the data in the third column (emergent dimensions of problems), from which six new and well-defined challenges emerged: the evaluation environment; bias and contradiction; responsibility for evaluation; quality of evaluation data; generational reach; and time expectation management. We have reimagined barriers as challenges to reflect their more positive connotations for opportunities to develop, rather than hinder, evaluation, despite the continued need for the evaluator to navigate skilfully and with care. This process effectively breaks down evaluation challenges into recognizable real-life experiences, from which

Table 13 Six new dimensions for evaluation challenges (with previous assumptions of barriers included) and their implications for leadership coaching and basic evaluation targets, resulting from the second application of levers

New evaluation challenge (assumed barriers)	Dimensions of leadership coaching	Influencing evaluation levers	Ambidextrous framework for evaluation target
Evaluation environment (strategic alignment and intangibles)	Managing tension between exploitative and explorative outcomes: in the context of a dominant primary goal	Primary goals Organizational context	Balancing performance with competitive relevance in the context of managing risk

Table 13   (Continued)

New evaluation challenge (assumed barriers)	Dimensions of leadership coaching	Influencing evaluation levers	Ambidextrous framework for evaluation target
Bias and contradiction (strategic alignment and intangibles)	Reward and recognition systems: emphasizing primary goal **Discretionary judgements: personal or departmental for financial interest** Strategic competence **Operational competence** Coaching efficacy: advocacy misuse for marketing **Interpretation: of outcomes of data**	Primary goals Evaluation status Organizational context	**Balancing internal budgetary justification with a culture of collective understanding in the context of managing strategic alignment** Balancing coaching efficacy with a fuller range of coaching outcomes in the context of managing professional judgement **Balancing RoI with well-being in the context of managing professional judgement**
Responsibility for evaluation (strategic alignment)	Proprietorial interest **Confused interest** The gap between operational and strategic approaches: what is stated as valued and what is being evaluated	Primary goals Evaluation status Organizational context	Balancing internal budgetary justification with a culture of collective understanding in the context of managing strategic alignment **Balancing a complex environment with opportunity generation in the context of managing change**

(Continued)

Table 13   (Continued)

New evaluation challenge (assumed barriers)	Dimensions of leadership coaching	Influencing evaluation levers	Ambidextrous framework for evaluation target
Quality of evaluation data (intangibles)	**Equivalent of Kirkpatrick's levels 1–4: self-informing, anecdotal, informal** Disconnected competency and assessment frameworks: run in parallel	Evaluation status Organizational context	Balancing coaching efficacy with a fuller range of coaching outcomes **Balancing RoI with well-being and engagement in the context of managing professional judgement**
Generational reach (contingencies)	**Flawed succession strategy** Retention of future leadership talent pools	Multigenerational leadership pools Organizational context	Balancing management with leadership perspectives in the context of managing social integration and relationships **Balancing efficiency savings with talent management for pivotal roles in the context of managing multiple structures**
Time expectation management (intangibles)	**Evaluation over time: for impact of coaching on leadership behaviours** Leadership transiency: continuity of coaching	Primary goals Organizational context	Balancing coaching efficacy with a fuller range of coaching outcomes

implications for leadership coaching can be drawn. In this developed table we begin to shift the emphasis away from challenges, towards leadership: outcomes and coaching. In this way, challenges have become a context for leadership coaching. Applying levers for a second time, to the emergent dimensions for coaching (real-life experiences), allows us to start to design evaluation targets using the ambidextrous framework.

An at-a-glance practitioner guide to using Tables 12 and 13

Figure 7: Using Table 12 to rationalize evaluation problematics and signpost leadership outcomes and coaching foci by placing them in an ambidextrous context

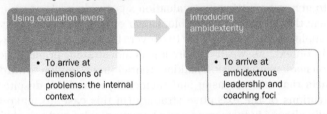

Figure 8: Using Table 13 to arrive at six new dimensions for evaluation challenges, to develop a context for leadership outcomes and coaching, and applying levers to produce basic evaluation targets

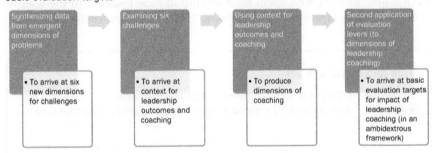

An in-depth examination of the six challenges to evaluation

As we have seen, assumptions can be casually used as convenient building blocks for theory. Accordingly, it would be remiss of us not to spend a bit of time analysing our six new challenges, not least to assess the advancement in our knowledge, facilitated by the application of evaluation levers and ambidexterity, delimiting the conventional wisdom that has previously held back progress in this area.

- **The evaluation environment**

So far, we have suggested that the evaluation environment has been a research rather than a practice issue. A lack of progress in evaluation has been attributed, in part, to the unambitious approach from researchers, constrained by a sense of obligation to produce actionable and measurable theory, but focused on operational or managerialist stakeholders. In mitigation, it might be claimed that leadership outcomes and their development, as described in our opening chapter, are in a constant state of evolutionary flux and that theorists have not caught up, continuing to work within the bounds of conceived HR wisdom, at a time when leadership development is transitioning rapidly from an operational to a strategic emphasis. What we have now learnt is that evaluation needs to be as agile and adaptive as the leadership strategies it serves.

In the context of a challenge, the evaluation environment simply means the organizational landscape in which evaluation takes place. Whether or not we are able to achieve an effective evaluation system depends on an evaluation environment that either enables or blocks our efforts. In this specific organizational example we found there were two levers in play: primary goals and organizational context. As we have already demonstrated, primary goals heap pressure on leadership decision-making, reorienting attention towards exploitative targets that can be easily and financially measured, despite the best-stated intentions of the executive strategy (in this case, to make balanced, strategically aligned judgements focused on intangibles and soft skills, as part of a subordinate strategy for talent management for high performance). As we have also seen, organizational context is an influence with a mind of its own, characterized by values, philosophies, historic attitudes and a default position for the practitioners who claim their organization is resistant to the idea of evaluation. Here, levers interact to create a difficult environment for evaluation.

Tips and exercises 23

Reflective exercise | Thinking of a current or recent coaching intervention, how has the environment for coaching changed or adapted during that time?

In what ways have the changes in the environment influenced how you coach, and how might you need to adapt your thinking about evaluating the impacts of your coaching?

- **Bias and contradiction**

The CIPD's (2008, 2014) assessment of evaluation as a loop is an idea we developed in the last chapter, in the context of describing primary goals as one of our four key influencers. The CIPD's more general concept referred to a connection between the unique definitions of value outcomes to appropriate and relevant metrics. Our experience challenged the CIPD's assertion as being only half right: an interesting dichotomy rather than an assured statement of fact. What we found was so-called unique definitions of value were inhibiting the pursuit of 'appropriate and relevant metrics', sitting at the heart of the evaluation paradox: what participants claim as being of value was not the focus for evaluation.

Despite their commitment to the new style of leadership, through transformational leadership programmes and leadership competency frameworks, in reality, stakeholders were setting evaluation up to fail. Accompanying performance management reviews and appraisals (a potential source for evaluation data) were found to be inextricably linked to reward and recognition systems, focused on financial self-interest, overriding the creative leadership strategies, of which stakeholders claimed to be so proud. Accordingly, there was no place for evaluation of these new behaviours and, in turn, leadership focus inevitably strayed away from intangibles and the soft skills developed by their coaches, where there was low financial legitimacy, despite evidence of their high strategic credentials. The CIPD's reference to 'unique definitions of value' actually meant the subjective judgements of different individual leaders, shaped by their attitude to personal remuneration, distorted 'relevant metrics' accordingly, as either inconsistent or wide of the target for overarching strategy. Therefore, far from being the catalyst for evaluation the CIPD envisioned, the primary goal, as the primary definition of value, facilitated by systems, judgements or advocacy that bypassed explorative outcomes, was in reality a source of bias and contradiction.

Evaluation status was the second lever we used to unlock this challenge. At one level, evaluation status has been characterized by the failure of human resource management to have evolved as a strategic function, resulting in evaluation metrics that contradict overarching strategy. However, our research found this was a far more complicated area, and to characterize it solely as the disconnect between operational and strategic arms of the organization is a too simplistic representation. Our research uncovered another complex level that needed to be taken into consideration, namely, the personality of those undertaking the evaluation, whether formal or informal status, was found to be a further source of inconsistent data. Evaluation is not yet a science, and however sophisticated or well supervised a system is, it is still reliant on the discretionary judgements of evaluators and their own personal agendas and insecurities. Lastly, organizational context was considered the undefined evaluation lever interacting with this challenge, overlapping with its two counterparts. Its inclusion in all six challenges reflects its overarching influence as a constant presence, representing the internal context.

A third classification for bias was found to emanate from coaching advocacy, specifically where evaluation formed part of the coaching contract or was put forward as an endorsement of coaching credentials. Somewhat comfortingly, a sizeable minority of our coach sample called out this practice and were sceptical about tendentious evaluator motives, which they saw as an 'abuse of trust'.

Tips and exercises 24

Reflective exercise

Returning to your own example above, where the coaching environment changed: how might these changes have shaped the impacts of the coaching?

Similarly, what are the implications of the wider environmental changes on the trustworthiness or credibility of the results? For example, what else has happened which may have had a more significant role in creating the results you have measured through the evaluation?

- **Responsibility for evaluation**

It was becoming apparent, as we unpacked our six challenges, that our evaluation inhibitors were distinguished by their multifaceted nature. In other words, evaluators would be making a fundamental error if they tried to take challenges at face value. To produce a practical and strategic system, practitioners would need to work hard to get beneath the skin of the organization to understand its layered complexity, selecting levers (more than one) skilfully, to unlock an understanding of the unique needs of the client. It is when we allow levers to interact that we achieve a eureka moment, and the components of an evaluation framework fall neatly into place. For instance, applying the evaluation status lever to the *responsibility for evaluation* challenge will show how evaluation data becomes distorted, limited or invalid, depending on formal or informal approaches. It is when we simultaneously apply the primary goal and organizational context levers that we get a true picture of the complex disconnect between formal and informal; strategic and operational; structured and discretionary, evaluation status.

The confusion over the responsibility for evaluation (see *The immiscible environment* Chapter 3 and *Evaluation: whose responsibility is it anyway?* Chapter 4) arguably reflects the low-grade importance attached to it by professionals. Furthermore, where responsibility was accepted, motives were often found to be impure: proprietorial, shaped and influenced by self-interest emanating from a primary goal. More generally, where lines of accountability for evaluating were blurred, it was likely that evaluation would fall between the cracks of the internal context and get ignored altogether.

Tips and exercises 25

Reflective
exercise

What practices or guidance do you currently have in place to ensure there is clear ownership of each stage of coaching and evaluation processes? Reflect on who owns each of the following steps of the coaching and evaluation processes, noting any ambiguities:

Commissioning:

Negotiating:

Contracting:

Communicating:

Evaluation scoping:

Evaluation implementation:

Evaluation write-up and sanctioning:

Snowballing:

Promotions:

- **Quality of evaluation data**

Our research experiences emboldened us to make the sweeping statement that, even if organizations get as far as evaluation, the data they retrieve is likely to be suboptimal and unreliable. In Chapter 1, we provided evidence of the lack of strategic ambition organizations and coaches showed for evaluation. Our headline findings (reassuringly from a research perspective, or disappointingly from a practice point of view) corresponded with the practice research that found only 7 per cent of organizations intended to evaluate the wider impact of leadership coaching on the business or society (CIPD 2015). Our research revealed participants primarily collected evaluation data to inform reward and recognition systems, or operational coaching dimensions (reflecting evaluation status and organizational context levers in play). As well as the strategic limitations of these evaluation targets, we also found data-collection methods characterized poor-quality data, inasmuch as most respondents were reliant on anecdotal or peer-review evidence to inform, often misaligned, evaluation targets.

An ever-present subtext for evaluation data is return on investment. RoI, often regarded as synonymous with evaluation, divides opinion: for and against, ranging from a 'benchmark for quality data' to a contrived and complicated set of calculations with little credibility, inappropriate to the coaching methodology. What is clear is, whichever school of thought the evaluator adopts, both have the capacity to derail evaluation.

Tips and exercises 26

Tip   *Data quality is not necessarily an intrinsic quality – the requirements for 'trustworthiness' and 'robustness' can depend on the scale and significance of the decision or action that will be taken as a result of the findings. This might be, for example, the amount of money that will be spent or the number of people affected by the coaching (or indeed, the number of people that could be negatively or positively affected by the findings). The evidence triangle is often referred to in coaching psychology circles.*

• **Generational reach**

In the last chapter, we made the claim that this is a pivotal moment for evaluation, not least because of the seismic shift in the generational workforce: as one generation retires, another succeeds, and one waits impatiently in the wings. However, as with other challenges, this is a far more intricate puzzle to solve than simply accommodating an unfamiliar set of new generational expectations. Unsurprisingly, the multigenerational leadership pool lever is dominant here; however, the organizational context is also a significant influencer, moving the evaluator beyond the obvious challenge to recognize and understand the logic of generational traits.

Working in concert, these levers expose the impact of self-interested individuals, in terms of their generational status, despite the best intentions of stakeholders and systems designed to counter bias and contradiction. For instance, in one example of a participating private sector partnership, the organizational context requires partners to retire at 60, reported as a deliberate facilitator for succession. However, in reality, incumbent leadership was reported to be 'protective and insecure' around succession, and focused on exploitative outcomes in recognition of what they perceived (the requirement to retire at 60) as a cap on earning potential. Flawed succession was also found to be connected to retention, and most participants reported deliberate attempts to retain top talent through distinct coaching programmes and lateral moves, to counter a lack of promotional opportunities.

The dedicated efforts to retain future leadership talent generations was reported to be a critical point of focus for all organizations participating in our research; however, using leadership coaching as a marker for a future leadership role, to encourage top talent to stay in the organization, was found to be extremely problematic for evaluation in terms of intangible explorative behaviours and skills, and indeterminate timelines.

- **Time expectation management**

The conventional definition for managing expectations in the context of time, references the leader's challenge to be ambidextrous, and the tension between leadership outcomes, increasingly characterized by long-term goals, and evaluation targets continuously focused on short-term impact. The failure for evaluators to rise to this challenge may, in part, be down to the widely held assumption that leadership is an enigmatic function, which they struggle to evaluate in the here and now; therefore, the prospect of revisiting the impact of leadership coaching, say five years on, is inconceivable.

However, as with our other evaluation challenges, we found a more complex dimension for time, triggered by the primary goal and organizational context levers, the implications of which support our claim, developing the discussion in Chapter 3, that practitioners will fail at evaluation if they take a one-size-fits-all approach. For instance, one organization's belief that top talent has a short shelf life in a fast-moving business, places capacity building, previously assumed to be a long-term explorative outcome, in a short-term exploitative context. This contrasts with the experiences of another organization, who see leadership as a consequence of long-term commitment, and struggle with a talent pool they consider to be disloyal or fickle, anticipating frequent career moves, with no intention of building a career in one place. Either way, these new dimensions illustrate the need for the coach to provide an agile offering, moving between not only distinct leadership cohorts, but also different industry attitudes to leadership and time expectations.

New knowledge and assumption-busting principles

Even a thumbnail sketch of this new set of challenges reveals a far more complicated landscape for evaluation than previously thought; therefore, it is probably not surprising that, given the limited knowledge available, practitioners have failed to find a formula for a workable and strategically useful system. Now, the question is, how do we use this new knowledge in the design of such a model? We should start by recognizing that, in the pursuit of knowledge, we have arrived at three assumption-busting principles as a foundation upon which to build our evaluation system.

- Existing ambidextrous frameworks, despite the exclusion of an evaluation function, contradict assumptions that intangible explorative outcomes are unmanageable or require a contrived, or overly complex, system for evaluation.

- Poor-quality data is sourced from the internal context, specifically structures such as reward and recognition systems, or from the influence of operational or strategic stakeholders, rather than faults in the design of evaluation approaches.
- Existing operational and conceptual ambidextrous balance mechanisms support the 'logic' element of evaluation, where previously it was claimed that organizations could not explain the connection between leadership behaviours and strategic success.

Tips and exercises 27

Tip   *Logic models are frequently assumed in evaluation – often used to explain (the 'logic' or 'theory') between an intervention (or set of activities) and measured resultant changes. However, in practice, the logic is often assumed or implied (also see theory of change, logic models of evaluation, and social return on investment).*

Free from the assumptions that fuelled evaluation failings, we are able to apply our two tools (levers and ambidexterity) to the design and build of a compelling evaluation model. Initially, the application of levers will allow us to explore the evaluation context, and compile an inventory of needs for the components of a workable system; then, using ambidexterity, we will unlock evaluation targets that are relevant and informative.

Evaluation stage 2 – Applying evaluation levers to the unique internal context (for the components of a workable system)

One of the fundamental principles of our evaluation model is that it cannot be simply 'taken off the shelf', but should be adaptable to the organization's DNA. Accordingly, we have seen how the application of levers has given us access to all areas of the unique internal context. Now, we apply levers again to what we have found out about the internal context for evaluation, to uncover the organization's blind spots and subsequent needs, for conversion into the components of a workable system. Using our example organization (private sector for profit), Table 14 demonstrates how levers illuminate blind spots, from which an inventory of needs is derived, to be used by the evaluator in the design of an evaluation system.

In this particular example, an effective evaluation model will need to be able to legitimize espoused (included in either operational or conceptual balance

Table 14 Applying levers to arrive at an inventory of needs

Evaluation lever	Definition	Blind spot	Inventory of needs
Primary goal	Financial performance for profit	Focus on short-term profit	Legitimization
Evaluation status	Informal	Inconsistent subjective judgements from directors motivated by financial self-interest	Undistorted data
Multigenerational leadership pools	• Retention of leadership talent • Succession	• Clear career paths • Succession strategy focused on short-term financial performance	• Distinct timelines • Focus on succession
Culture	Executive directors	• Individual interpretations • Inherent beliefs and values undermining modernizing strategies of questionable financial legitimacy	Consistent judgement

mechanisms) long-term leadership coaching outcomes (emphasizing talent management), by placing them in the context of a primary goal for profit, in a way that is clearly understood by the leader and reciprocated in terms of performance management. It will also need to untangle potentially distorted data, either at the source (the evaluator) or through some form of weighting system that rewards and recognizes indirect financial contribution. In addition, it will need to recognize that one of the key leadership outcomes, the retention of talent, is under pressure from incumbent leadership, reluctant to fully commit to a succession strategy due to self-interest. Therefore, any evaluation model will need to consider various leadership hierarchies and accompanying timelines, to make the case for selfless succession, simultaneously retaining and attracting upcoming leadership talent. Finally, the evaluation design should either make allowances for, or provide a correcting device for, inconsistent subjective judgements from evaluators with different motivations, or who undermine the overarching strategy through an inherent set of beliefs and values that characterize the governance of the organization.

This process addresses one of our early presumptive questions and shows why it would not be feasible to simply extend existing ambidextrous frameworks to include evaluation, however convenient that notion might appear. The evaluator should invest time in applying evaluation levers to interact with the organizational DNA and understand its specific needs to produce a tailor-made blueprint for evaluation. It also exposes the flawed thinking behind any evaluation approach that does not go to similar lengths to adapt evaluation to the unique internal context.

Evaluation stage 3 – Applying ambidexterity to the organizational strategy (for relevant and strategically informative data)

This book has been well served by ambidexterity. Initially, we used it as a lens through which to examine evaluation, as a way of replicating the complex and dynamic organizational context within which leaders currently operate. Serendipitously, we then discovered that organizations were familiar with the concept of ambidexterity, through various existing strategies to promote a new style of leadership (and accompanying coaching dimensions), to achieve high-level performance. Finally, we intend to use ambidexterity as our second tool (after levers) to facilitate our claim that any evaluation system needs to not only work, but be strategically useful, to fully incentivize organizations to take notice. Here, we are looking to ambidexterity to unlock the strategic potential of our evaluation model.

Before we put ambidexterity to work again, let us take a step back and explain how ambidexterity appears as part of an organization's leadership strategy. In the graphic (Figure 9), we have imagined ambidextrous strategy as part of the organizational DNA (internal context), as a double helix, emphasizing that it is not a simple binary concept, but a subtle collaboration between exploitative and explorative leadership outcomes. To give structure (strategic alignment) to the idea of tangible and intangible outcomes working in harmony, we found organizations connected these by building chains of impact for subordinate strategies (facilitated by operational and conceptual balance mechanisms) to achieve a primary goal.

Figure 9 illustrates the strategic credentials of ambidexterity, and supports the claim that it is well placed as a source for valuable strategic insights. Attaching ambidexterity to evaluation gives it a convenient vehicle to function

Figure 9: Exploitative and explorative leadership outcomes strategically aligned to achieve a primary goal

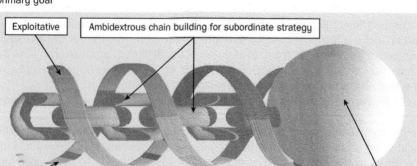

as a strategic informant, simultaneously bolstering the case for evaluation. In the next chapter, this point is emphasized in the section that suggests three fundamental principles for evaluation, highlighting the importance of integrating any evaluation model precisely, into the strategic chain.

Having provided an understanding of the practical evaluation needs of the organization, we now have the opportunity to use ambidexterity as a tool, to deliver the valuable insights into an unfamiliar, wider strategy, characterized by innovation and creativity, that organizations crave. Using our organizational context guinea pig, we start by breaking down the subordinate strategy, in this case, broadly defined as talent management for high performance. To do this, we begin by identifying the component parts of the strategic chain, as potential evaluation metrics, the data from which will go on to inform a strategic goal.

Table 15 illustrates the final phase for evaluation, focusing evaluation needs, as responses to blind spots and the necessary components for a workable

Table 15 Using ambidexterity to redirect resultant data to strategic targets

Inventory of needs	Subordinate strategy and timeline for primary goal	Exploitative chain link: evaluation target	Explorative chain link: evaluation target	To strategically inform
Legitimization	Long-term capacity building for growth	Short-term known (financially) outcomes for continuous profitability	Long-term unknown (financially) outcomes	Long-term growth strategy by providing short-term financial assurance
Undistorted data	Strategic alignment	Reward	Recognition	Reward and recognition that recognizes the wider leadership contribution
Distinct timelines Focus on succession	Recruitment, development and retention of top talent	Allocation of talent to high-impact roles	Development of talent and internal coaching	Recruitment strategy, including attracting talent Retention strategy, including generational needs Succession strategy
	Succession	Managing out	Managing up: transforming attitudes	
Consistent judgement	Modernizing attitudes to leadership and governance	Distinct leadership roles for directors as part of a governance transformation strategy	Modernizing culture, creating a new leadership environment of collective understanding	Modernizing and transformational strategy

system, on the specific ambidextrous elements of a subordinate strategy, to redirect resultant evaluation data to inform strategy. In this demonstration, say, a system that recognizes an organizational vulnerability to produce distorted data will now have the capability to isolate those elements, by connecting them to the subordinate ambidextrous strategy and placing them in the spotlight of leadership expectations (i.e. evaluation targets). The emergent evaluation data is then redirected to inform reward and recognition systems, to assure they are effectively strategically aligned in the future.

In this chapter, we have provided a demonstrable guide for the construction of a practical evaluation system by using levers and, through the application of ambidexterity, we have signposted the potential strategic usefulness of any such system. However, throughout this book, we have been at pains to emphasize that evaluation is a complex puzzle, constantly evolving, buzzing with new ideas around leadership and coaching. Therefore, in search of a simple, elegant evaluation process, we must first accept its layers of complication and those unexpected contingencies thrown up by the idiosyncrasies of the organization. Not to do so will mean the evaluator is liable to fall short, when building their model, of putting these new ideas into real practice.

Summary of key points

This chapter converts new knowledge into practical tools for evaluation. Levers are applied to provide a real understanding of barriers, reimagined as challenges, by unlocking the evaluation needs of the organization's unique internal context, to produce the component parts of a workable system. Ambidexterity is then used to highlight the strategic destination of resultant evaluation data. In this process, evaluation levers are applied three times: to set the context for evaluation; to connect emergent challenges, in the context of coaching dimensions, to potential evaluation targets; and to produce an inventory of needs for an effective system design. Ambidexterity is then introduced to clarify leadership and coaching targets for evaluation, simultaneously guiding the destination of data to strategically valuable hotspots.

Chapter tool/template

Tool (for personal and team practice):

Evaluation levers (personal and team reflection)

This template tool encourages proactive thinking about leadership coaching design and implementation using levers.

Step 1: Reflect through the different aspects of the levers, working from left to right on the table below. Add details of the specific organization or context in which the evaluation is to take place.

Evaluation lever	Definition	Blind spots	Inventory of needs	Action to address need
Primary goal	Financial performance for surplus/profit	Focus on short-term profit	Legitimization	
	Specific organizational goals: • • •	Specific blind spots: • • •	Specific needs (if any): • • •	
Evaluation status in the organization/unit where evaluation needs to have an influence	Informal	Inconsistent subjective judgements from stakeholders with different motivations	Undistorted data	
	Specific notes about evaluation in the context: • • •	Specific blind spots: • • •	Specific needs (if any): • • •	
Multigenerational leadership pools – patterns and issues	Retention of leadership talent	Clear career paths	Distinct timelines	
	Succession	Succession strategy	Focus on succession	

Evaluation lever	Definition	Blind spots	Inventory of needs	Action to address need
	Specific patterns and issues to address: • • •	Specific blind spots: • • •	Specific needs (if any): • • •	
Organizational context	Executive board	Distinct stakeholder attitudes to the running of the business Inherent beliefs and values undermining modernizing strategies	Consistent judgement	
	Specific cultural ways of operating: • • •	Specific blind spots: • • •	Specific needs (if any): • • •	

Step 2: Reflect on the table to identify any tensions and discuss these to identify any reconciliations with decision-makers (where possible). Bear in mind the principle of parsimony, or the least number of working parts to achieve the ultimate aim.

Evaluation lever	Definition	Blind spots	Inventory of needs	Action to address need
Primary goal				
Evaluation status in the organization				
Multigenerational leadership pools				
Organizational context				

6 How to evaluate: Part 2 – Building an evaluation system

Chapter in brief

This chapter moves to build an integrated, multipurpose prototype evaluation model. Initially, it returns to address the reality that, for any evaluation system to be truly effective, evaluators and stakeholders need to find the will to evaluate. From an exploration of this delicate philosophical question it offers up the idea of *unknowns* as a practical interpretation of a nebulous concept from which three provocations are revealed, designed to stimulate practitioners to adopt a meaningful interest in evaluation. It then goes on to examine existing concepts (what organizations already have in place) as seven promising movements for evaluation. From these movements, three ideas emerge as foundational principles upon which to build our evaluation model: expand, integrate and collaborate. Finally, it presents a blueprint for a workable model that includes the capability to provide focus for coaching outcomes, relevant evaluation metrics, and a logical destination for resultant data.

Introducing evaluation provocations: presenting *unknowns* as a strategic stimulant

As the research for this book developed, so did its subtext, and we quickly realized that the simple *guide for professionals* we had envisaged would not best serve our readers. The subtext to which we refer is the intellectual dimension of the problematic nature of evaluation: regardless of theories, systems and evidence, do evaluators actually have the will to evaluate? We felt that if we could understand more about the philosophy of evaluation we would be acknowledging an unknown, overlooked element that would help us close the gap between theory and practice. Without this piece of the jigsaw, our work would be incomplete. At the same time, we believed that if we could harness these elements we might add insights to the contradictions, dichotomies and paradoxes that characterize evaluation. Accordingly, to make them work for us, we conveniently classified the components of this particular puzzle as *unknowns* and included them in our formulations.

These *unknowns*, or a version of them, have already played a significant role in our understanding of the internal context, highlighting the intangible characteristics of the organization that impact evaluation: attitudes, preju- dices, philosophies, inherent values, cynicism, etc. However, at this stage, as we prepare to build our evaluation model, *unknowns* are a more urgent, nebu- lous concept that we have no real way of accommodating in our design calcu- lations (unlike other intangibles, where we have provided practical legitimacy, isolating their contribution to a primary goal). We decided we had two choices with *unknowns*: we could casually overlook them as part of the idiosyncratic nature of evaluation, or we could put them to work by reimagining them as a series of provocations, emphasizing evaluation as a strategy, as opposed to an operational task. In adopting the latter, we found a series of provocations, use- ful to our quest, acting as a catalyst for design and a stress test for coaching motivations.

Three evaluation provocations

Provocation 1: Strategic investment to achieve high performance through transformational and expensive leadership coaching programmes is insuffi- cient, unaccompanied by a commitment to examine and simultaneously trans- form the internal context where necessary.

Provocation 2: The evidence that evaluation provides the advocacy and tools to make a valuable strategic contribution asks questions of both coach and stakeholder/client who choose to ignore its potential.

Provocation 3: If a collaborative relationship is unachievable, does this compromise the coach offering, and at what stage should the coach reject the contract?

Tips and exercises 28

Tip *A 'provocation' has the intent to make us think, connect previously unconnected dots, to find our own answers. The idea behind a provocation – linking back to our working model idea – is that we become accustomed to a dynamic and evolving way of practising coaching and coaching evaluation. And this loops us back to the need to be able to deal with uncertainty.*

Reflective What are your current thoughts in relation to the provocations
exercise below:

Provocation 1: Strategic investment to achieve high performance through transformational and expensive leadership coaching pro- grammes, is insufficient, unaccompanied by a commitment to examine and simultaneously transform the internal context where necessary.

Provocation 2: The evidence that evaluation provides the advocacy and tools to make a valuable strategic contribution, asks questions of both coach and stakeholder/client who choose to ignore its potential.

Provocation 3: If a collaborative relationship is unachievable, does this compromise the coach offering, and at what stage should the coach reject the contract?

As practitioners reading this book, we urge you not to simply follow the guidelines we have laid down for a compelling evaluation model; success requires you to address *unknowns*. In other words, organizations need to be prepared, and helped, to dismantle existing structures and ingrained mindsets; close the ideological gap between strategic and operational thinking; find ways to negate financial self-interest; bust silo mentalities, and provide a psychologically secure environment for evaluation. The idea of *unknowns* challenges our assertion that evaluation influencers are solely in the hands of the stakeholder, providing an additional, complex psychological dimension to the internal context. However, converting *unknowns* to tactical provocations, as part of the evaluation process, will act as a strategic stimulant, and a trigger for organizations to re-examine their internal context, to better understand their idiosyncrasies and facilitate an effective strategic evaluation approach. Having risen to this challenge, we are now ready to build our evaluation system.

How to build an evaluation system

What we already have: the seven promising movements for evaluation

Our book highlights the contrast between the revolution in leadership and coaching and the gradual evolution of evaluation. However, as we set about building our evaluation system, we should not be wholly reliant on analysing what has gone wrong, or what is absent, but also recognize the existence of promising movements (what we already have that works) and their potential contribution. Accordingly, we found seven concepts, systems and strategies, underused or disregarded in the context of evaluation, that were of interest, as we accumulated knowledge to formulate our system.

1 Universal ambidexterity: the key that unlocked the new strategic mindset

Our use of ambidexterity as a research context, a strategic stimulus and, finally, an evaluation tool, has been well documented. However, the discovery that ambidexterity was universally accepted as a strategic opportunity should not be underestimated as a part of our process, and was another eureka moment for our study. When we presented ambidexterity as a research context to our stakeholders, we quickly latched on to the positive familiarity with which strategists responded, which for us was a key path, connecting evaluation to strategy. Ambidexterity has emerged as a strategic response to an increasingly dynamic organizational context, making sense of conflicting external pressures and creating a seedbed for creative and innovative solutions. It has enabled organizations to cope with unpredictable contingencies outside their control, negating these as inhibitors of evaluation and, at the same time, expanding the discussion around evaluation to include strategic dimensions.

2 Chain building – operational and conceptual balance mechanisms

What we came to realize, as our research unfolded, was that organizations already have in place evaluation templates; they just do not include evaluation. Universal awareness of the strategic opportunities from ambidexterity acted as a driver for what we have described as operational and conceptual balance mechanisms. Balance mechanisms were found to encapsulate the emerging leadership mindset and coaching outcomes, in a deliberate attempt to cultivate a consensus of purpose, by promoting the behavioural integration necessary to align the new complexities of strategy.

These balance mechanisms are discussed in detail in Chapter 2 but, in summary, connecting intangible outcomes to tangible targets through various frameworks provided practitioners with an opening to evaluate coaching impact on explorative leadership outcomes by placing them in an exploitative context for inclusion in internal performance management systems. We found balance mechanisms were another enabling factor in our quest to connect evaluation to strategy, designating clearly aligned strategic targets as a key driver for evaluation. However, we have also, more recently, posited that the complexity and unpredictability of the internal context, and the presence of *unknowns*, is liable to prevent a straightforward expansion of existing frameworks to include evaluation, although these may be a good place to start.

3 Demystifying soft skills for hard evaluation

Unfamiliar intangible soft-skill outcomes have always perplexed evaluators as one of the three main preconceptions contributing to the self-fulfilling prophecy that confines evaluation practice to mainly irrelevant, operational targets. However, we found evidence that existing ambidextrous frameworks (see balance mechanisms above) acted as deliberate strategies to explain unknown intangible leadership behaviours by placing them in the context of a primary goal, negating this as an assumed barrier to evaluation. As part of this deliberate strategy, organizations identified desired intangible leadership outcomes in named classifications as a way of demystifying the unfamiliar new expectations of leadership, connecting them to internal performance management systems. Organizations used creative language to classify soft-skilled leadership behaviours and thinking, such as *trusted partner, custodian* and *good citizen,* as a way of clarifying expectations and providing targets for leadership assessment. These catch-all categories are seen as a tactical response to the difficulty leaders have in identifying with intangible outcomes, specifically in terms of providing strategic legitimization through formal inclusion in appraisals. Where balance mechanisms provide a physical strategy to explain explorative outcomes, the tone and language adopted by organizations was found to supplement and support these strategies.

4 Reward and recognition

Leaders' reward and recognition systems sit at the heart of the paradoxical landscape for evaluation, distracting practitioners by being closely aligned to personal interest, distorting data, and as the chief architect of bias and inconsistency. However, we found evidence of organizations making attempts to recognize unknown values, through 'contingency rewards' (incentivized remuneration for a wider contribution – O'Reilly and Tushman 2004). Mostly, these efforts were overpowered by their relationship with performance targets, but we did find examples that some organizations were aware leaders' compensation systems conflicted with desired new behaviours, and they were making efforts to mitigate the impact of this association. The fact that some organizations are even thinking in this way, prepared to experiment with creative approaches to leaders' remuneration, was cause for optimism. For instance, we found one organization using an ambidextrous reward system, acknowledging both exploitative targets for performance (rewarded in cash), and explorative goals for future development and growth (rewarded in equity). This example suggests that accommodating contingency rewards need not overly tax the intellect of the organization.

5 Coaching for distinct leadership hierarchies

To differentiate between pivotal leadership roles and tiers, organizations used various versions of leadership hierarchies. Generally, these were designed as a tactical response to either accommodate and manage a large leadership cohort, or as part of a retention policy for high potentials where limited traditional leadership roles were available. From an evaluation point of view, distinct leadership hierarchies were helpful in a couple of ways. Firstly, they provided a reference point for varying evaluation metrics, by deconstructing leadership outcomes, to take into consideration different levels of expectations from distinct coaching interventions and timelines. Secondly, they have the potential to widen the context for leadership, uncovering multiple layers, often missed by evaluation theorists (who have a tendency to conveniently generalize leadership as a single entity), but highly relevant in the real world, particularly in public and third sector organizations. Expanding the scope of leadership in organizations also contributes to the reward and recognition process and strategies for retention of top talent (by providing clear leadership career pathways), and another potential destination for evaluation data as a strategic informant.

6 Demise of traditional performance reviews

Although evaluation has not kept pace with the revolution of leadership, thinking around traditional appraisals has been included in the transformational process. The demise of traditional appraisal formats and performance reviews is something both researchers and practitioners agree on. This change in tone, specifically the rigidity of structured reviews, more likely to be in the domain of the operational side of the organization, is a potential plus for the future of evaluation, loosening the grip of reward and recognition systems on leadership assessment.

7 The privileged position of the coach as evaluator

Perhaps unfairly, we have spent a disproportionately short time examining promising movements from the coach perspective. Having earlier dismissed (coach) attitudes to evaluation as largely tendentious, lacking both credibility (especially in terms of RoI) and strategic direction, we could also claim the responses from coaches were not particularly encouraging. Here, evaluation was either not seen as part of the coach offering, or described as a poor fit for the coaching philosophy. However, we have seen some cases of diligent collection of evaluation data from coach consultancies. Despite being thwarted at the dissemination stage, unable to contribute strategically useful data to the client, through internal systems and attitudes, these attempts at evaluation recognize the potentially privileged position of the coach, with access to a wealth of accumulated data across myriad diverse organizations, for valuable, insightful themes.

There were also hints that some coaches were becoming more aware of the need to be strategically aligned and relevant to the business needs of the client. Again, there was acknowledgement of the advantageous position held by the coach as an external influence, with access to both the executive and HR functions of the organization and, therefore, with the potential to actively narrow the gap between strategic and operational mindsets. Glimpses of positive evaluation attitudes from coaches suggest the benefits of a more active collaboration with the client, requiring the coach to develop, what Wall et al. (2017) describe as, professional judgement to make contextualized decisions which acknowledge the need for an intimate understanding of the cultural, historical and organizational context (the internal context).

These seven movements are tantalizing hints that suggest a workable and strategically valuable evaluation concept is within the grasp of practitioners. Our aim throughout this book has been to convince practitioners that evaluation is a strategic choice rather than an operational task, by neutralizing preconceptions about challenges and providing evidence of a wider strategic contribution, to make a compelling case. As we now build our model from an accumulation of new knowledge and insights, three new ideas emerge as foundational principles for our assemblage: expand, integrate and collaborate.

Tips and exercises 29

Tip
Professional judgement relates to your decision-making and brings together experiences of perceived similar situations or contexts. It can be expanded through lived experience, but also thought experiments which simulate conditions (e.g. reflection).

Reflective exercise
After reading about the emerging seven movements related to leadership coaching evaluation, which areas raise your curiosity in terms of your own practice?

1 Universal ambidexterity: the key that unlocked the new strategic mindset
2 Chain building – operational and conceptual balance mechanisms
3 Demystifying soft skills for hard evaluation
4 Reward and recognition
5 Coaching for distinct leadership hierarchies
6 Demise of traditional performance reviews
7 The privileged position of the coach as evaluator

For each area of curiosity, you can explore a thought experiment. For example, you might imagine a context with a specific:

- Organization:
- Setting:
- Location:
- Actors (e.g. commissioner, leader):
- Leadership role:
- Responsibility level/position in hierarchy:
- Leadership development issue:
- Financial standing of the organization:
- Sector:
- Economic climate:

How might your area of curiosity present in your imagination? What would you do in this thought experiment? Think through at least three steps of response or action.

The three foundational principles for an evaluation system (with accompanying provocations)

1 Expand existing ambidextrous frameworks to include new coaching dimensions and evaluation

We now know that organizations view ambidextrous frameworks as strategic mechanisms, incorporating transformational leadership thinking and behaviours, to build chains between exploitative and explorative targets as part of subordinate strategies towards a primary goal. Not only did these existing mechanisms emphasize leadership expectations, but they were found to successfully isolate the contribution of intangible outcomes, explaining their relevance by connecting them to strategy, thus neutralizing two out of the three persistently claimed barriers to evaluation: intangibles and strategic alignment (the third barrier according to practitioners, contingencies, having already been reassigned as an enabler rather than an inhibitor). We also discussed, in the last chapter, that to extend existing ambidextrous frameworks to include evaluation is too simplistic, due to the overriding influence of the internal context and the will of the organization to dismantle historic, cultural and 'political' barriers. Nevertheless, these frameworks are sufficient to set the tone for evaluation and form a basis for a workable system, especially after the application of our two evaluation tools, refocusing the design to consider the impact of unique internal faultlines.

We would also suggest that, not only do these frameworks have the potential to provide a focus for evaluation, they also come with an opportunity to include coaching dimensions as part of an integrated strategy, bringing together leadership, leadership development and evaluation, under the umbrella of the wider organizational strategy. Table 15 at the end of the last chapter is a good example of an ambidextrous template, specifically directing the attention of the evaluator to the strategically informant potential of evaluation. However, an additional column might easily be included (Table 16 below), identifying specific coaching outcomes (to be agreed between, and completed by, the individual leader, the coach and the stakeholder): strategically aligned and in touch with the constantly moving target of leadership in a dynamic environment.

Accompanying provocation

Organizational stakeholders and coaches view leadership coaching as delivering a strategic priority; at the same time, they treat its evaluation as low strategy status, instead, focusing on cost and operational accountability. This approach ignores the opportunity to elicit important insights to inform a highly prized, constantly evolving leadership strategy for high performance.

Are both (stakeholders and coaches) prepared to act on the implications of this dichotomy, that, without a re-examination (or in the case of the coach

Table 16 Reimagined framework for directing strategic data, including specific coaching outcomes for the individual leader

Inventory of needs	Subordinate strategy and timeline for primary goal	Exploitative chain link: evaluation target	Explorative chain link: evaluation target	Specific coaching outcomes (example)	To strategically inform
Legitimization	Long-term capacity building for growth	Short-term known (financially) outcomes for continuous profitability	Long-term unknown (financially) outcomes	*Judgement* *Prioritization* *Decision-making*	Long-term growth strategy by providing short-term financial assurance
Undistorted data	Strategic alignment	Reward	Recognition	*Confidence* *Vision*	Reward and recognition that recognizes the wider leadership contribution
Distinct timelines Focus on succession	Recruitment, development and retention of top talent	Allocation of talent to high-impact roles	Development of talent and internal coaching	*Manager coach behaviours* *Delegation* *Mentoring skills*	Recruitment strategy, including attracting talent Retention strategy, including generational needs
	Succession	Managing out	Managing up: transforming attitudes	*Talent development for succession* *Networking for recruitment*	Succession strategy
Consistent judgement	Modernizing attitudes to leadership and governance	Distinct leadership roles for directors as part of a governance transformation strategy	Modernizing culture creating a new leadership environment of collective understanding	*Team building* *Collective vision* *Communications*	Modernizing and transformational strategy

evaluator, an understanding) of the internal context, as an inhibitor of valuable strategic data, one of the organization's most significant investments is being self-sabotaged?

2 Integrate evaluation into a strategic chain

To expand the scope of evaluation data to be strategically incisive, we are proposing that any system needs to be integrated into the strategic chain, adhering to one of our guiding truths: connecting evaluation to strategy to elicit relevant information. In the example (Figure 10), we have inserted our evaluation framework between the organizational needs (the practical components of our system) and organizational balance mechanisms (the strategic focus for our system). Through this positioning, evaluation provides the link in the chain, connecting the internal context directly to the primary goal strategy. In terms of evaluation, this position allows our framework be informed by the internal context, for a workable system, simultaneously connecting resultant data to important strategic targets. We can see in the graphic (Figure 10) how positioning our evaluation framework is, in itself, a strategic decision.

The idea of integrating our system into the strategic chain makes a statement about the potential of evaluation as a strategic informant. However, placing it in a chain, as a separate link, or component, also provides an opportunity for the organization to include an independent (of dominant stakeholders and primary goals) function at the heart of their strategy structure. Furthermore, as an individual part, it is much more accessible to practitioners as part of the strategic engine that drives the organization. In this way, evaluators can isolate the evaluation component, effectively circuit-breaking the system, to use it in an adaptive way, appropriate to the needs of the organization at any given time, either as part of the process to inform a shift in the overarching strategy, or directly focused on a specific strategic target.

Figure 10: Where a framework for evaluation might sit in an ambidextrous chain-building strategy to achieve a primary goal

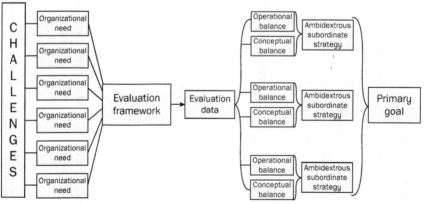

Accompanying provocation

Integrating evaluation into the wider strategic process effectively narrows the gap between operational and strategic functions. Accordingly, how willing are stakeholders to take on exposed blockers (operational and executive) to this integration where, not to do so, implies they are choosing to ignore a new source of valuable strategic balance for the sake of a potentially difficult conversation?

3 A new level of collaboration

Effective strategic collaboration between the coach and the client is rare. Our research from both perspectives provides evidence that, either individually or collectively, organizations and coaches are practically and intellectually inactive, at best reactive, in terms of evaluation. Informed by an inventory of needs, practitioners now have the opportunity to customize the design of any evaluation system emphasizing individual areas, designed and influenced by the unique internal context – thus illuminating blind spots and strategic leadership coaching targets, to be relevant and workable, and best serve the organizational purpose. However, having built a practical model, we should not simply assume that practitioners will go to the trouble of implementing it.

The execution of evaluation is a separate challenge, operationally and conceptually, and three main collaboration focal points to assist implementation emerged from our research: key relationships, the coach's role as an arbiter for evaluation, and the coach's input in the design of evaluation frameworks.

- **Key relationships**

In the hands of the coach, evaluation levers provide intimate independent access to the internal machinations of the organization, suggesting (possibly controversially) a new pivotal role for the coach as a quasi-consultant to the wider strategy, facilitated by strategically aligned evaluation data. We say controversial, because our research found that neither coaches nor organizational evaluation stakeholders necessarily welcomed an expansive role for an external consultant (coach), with responses ranging from 'inappropriate' to 'meddlesome'.

Dare we also suggest that it is incumbent on the coach to educate the organization through the terms and conditions of the coaching contract, seeking out a collaborative relationship with key stakeholders. In doing so, the coach would be able to make use of valuable insights (free from cultural sensitivities) of the internal context, to deliver focused strategically aligned coaching, integrating evaluation as a vital part of the offering. Alternatively, if the coach is not prepared to try to forge a key relationship, it must bring into question the veracity and effectiveness of the coaching offering, as well as the organization's selection process.

- **The coach as an arbiter for evaluation**

In recognizing the strategic potential of a collaborative relationship, the scope of collaboration now extends beyond simply sitting down together to agree outcomes. Having accepted a closer working relationship, there is now the opportunity to disambiguate multiple definitions and priorities for evaluation targets (a major source of bias and contradiction), and the effective dissemination (a persistent challenge) of relevant strategically aligned data. As an external consultant with an intimate knowledge of the internal context, the coach is in a position to make recommendations that negate bias and contradiction, bust departmental silos and neutralize inconsistent judgements arising from flawed succession planning, financial self-interest, misaligned operational perspectives and other *unknowns*.

- **The coach as co-designer for evaluation**

With the knowledge and tools now at the coach's disposal, coaches are ideally placed to extend their offering to assist in the design of bespoke systems that connect evaluation directly to strategy. Using a neutral perspective of the internal context, levers might be redeployed, as part of a practical collaboration, to design, or simply extend, ambidextrous frameworks, now positioned as an independent component of an integral (to the strategic chain) system.

Accompanying provocation

The conceptual dimension of the coach–client relationship is, arguably, more difficult to fathom. The use of levers as a tool for evaluation, and the insights and knowledge they produce, suggests the coach is qualified to make a wider contribution to the organization. At the same time, our research shows that organizations are often reluctant to countenance external input into existing internal contexts or executive strategy.

This stand-off raises a wider question which might involve difficult decisions about the future structure of the coaching contract, specifically: with what we now know about the potential strategic contribution of evaluation, if a collaborative relationship is unachievable, does this compromise the coach offering, and at what stage should the coach reject the contract for the sake of their professional integrity?

In this book we openly acknowledge that coaching is big business, and ambidexterity has exposed tensions between short-term financial gain and long-term professional integrity (similar to the tensions experienced by organizations). Without access to unique organizational systems and structures, we now have evidence that the coaching intervention, and let us not forget this forms a key strategy for leadership to deliver organizational primary goals, is liable to be restricted or limited, and at risk of disappointing all members of the tripartite (coach, sponsor, coachee) relationship.

Tips and exercises 30

Tip   *Involving stakeholders in the evaluation is common practice for some forms of evaluation (e.g.* social value assessment or social return on investment). *Doing so helps account for the notion of relative value – what I value might be very different to you. For example, I might want you to progress your leadership career and double your salary, but you might be more interested in saving lives. While we can spend time measuring your increase in salary, this is not a valued outcome to you or your organization.*

Reflective   Imagine one of your current clients standing in front of you. Imag-
exercise   ine the network of people who might have an interest in the outcomes of their coaching, in their widest ecosystem. List each of
their stakeholders, and then imagine what each of these might
value in terms of changes from the coaching. As you do this, note
what *additionally* you might learn from involving them in judging
or valuing the changes that occur as a result of your coaching.

Stakeholder	What changes the stakeholder might value	What I might learn – additionally – from involving them in the evaluation process

Bringing it all together: The end product

The dimensions of our prototype evaluation model (Table 17) are deliberately uncomplicated, focused on isolating the contributions of exploitative and explorative outcomes as part of a subordinate strategy for a primary goal. This is a blueprint and we expect various versions to emerge, particularly as we have worked hard to come up with a framework that is capable of being adapted to diverse, unique organizational contexts and needs. Whichever way it is fine-tuned, it is presented to the reader as a truly integrated, multipurpose evaluation system, connecting organizational strategies, coaching outcomes and evaluation (for the purpose of accountability and as a strategic informant), brought together in the same place, at the same time, to provide:

- A diagnostic tool for leadership coaching outcomes, focused on the most current and relevant targets in the context of a dynamic overarching strategy.
- An agile and purposeful focus for evaluation and evaluation metrics.
- A logical destination for resultant data as an informant for the current strategy.

The four case studies that comprise the final section of this book produce real-life applications of these ideas. However, we could not resist the opportunity to test drive our model, revisiting our example organization in Chapter 5 (a private sector organization focused on a primary goal for profit). In this demonstration (Table 18), evaluation is focused on exploitative and explorative leadership targets, reflecting the individual leader's areas for development (strengths and weaknesses). The balance of the framework is a response to the organization's inventory of needs, specifically: legitimization and undistorted data.

In this imagined example, the evaluation model recognizes three subordinate strategies for a primary goal: talent management, succession and high performance. Using evaluation levers, the organization's blind spots, subsequently formulated through an inventory of needs, provide the basis for a

Table 17 Prototype integrated evaluation framework

Subordinate strategy for primary goal	Exploitative leadership target	Explorative leadership target	Leadership coaching focus	Evaluation criteria	Strategic data

workable framework and an emphasis for evaluation focus to deliver a balanced approach. For instance, where legitimization (a leaning to short-term profit) has been flagged as a blind spot, evaluation has variously emphasized long-term expectations for growth, development and vision. Where undistorted data has been identified as a need, evaluation data has been diverted to inform reward and recognition systems in the context of succession. Through the application of ambidexterity, resultant data is channelled into strategic insights to inform current and future strategies. The individual development needs of the leader are reflected in the *leadership coaching focus* column, adding precision to the evaluation process and keeping it focused on the impact of the coaching.

Summary of key points

This chapter presents three provocations resulting from new knowledge, as an informal, additional tool, to stimulate practitioners to go beyond *unknowns* and adopt an active interest in evaluation. It then begins the practical process of building an evaluation model, starting with a summary of seven existing promising movements, disregarded or underused in the context of evaluation. From these, three fundamental principles emerge to assist in the design of our model: expand, integrate and collaborate (using provocations as a subtext for each principle to stimulate discussion). Finally, we present a prototype evaluation model practically designed around the organization's inventory of needs, that provides: a diagnostic tool for coaching outcomes, an agile focus for evaluation and a logical destination for data to inform strategic targets.

Table 18   Example of evaluation model at work (reflecting organizational needs for legitimization and undistorted data)

Subordinate strategy for primary goal	Exploitative leadership target	Explorative leadership target	Leadership coaching focus	Evaluation criteria	Strategic data
Talent management	Recruitment and retention	Attracting and motivating top talent	Coaching behaviours	Recruitment **Promotions** Retention **Development** (of associated teams or individuals)	General needs **Recruitment strategy** Pivotal posts **Future development programmes**
Succession	Seamless transition **Deep leadership pool**	Developing high potentials **Managing high potentials**	Managing internal relationships **Managing self** Managing expectations	Identification and ongoing development of successor **Personal development as custodian of the business** Identify leadership pathway design **Long-term assessment**	Exit strategies **Lateral moves across organization** Leadership pathways **Transforming leadership (new outcomes)** Reward and recognition
High performance	Delivering targets	Unlocking discretionary energy	Coaching behaviours **Motivational tools** Ambidextrous judgements	Financial targets **Vision (business ideas)**	Future income budgets **Creative strategies** Growth capacity

Chapter tool/template

Tool (for personal practice):

Mapping an integrated leadership coaching evaluation framework (personal reflection)

This template tool encourages proactive thinking about how to design an integrated leadership coaching framework.

The first step involves reflecting through the different columns in the table below, working on the table from left to right. Ensure you and others using the table are specific about the organization or context in which the evaluation is to take place. The final column maps out which standard, practical data-collection methods and tools will collect the data. Bear in mind the principle of parsimony, or the least number of working parts to achieve the ultimate aim.

Subordinate strategy for primary goal	Exploitative leadership target	Explorative leadership target	Leadership coaching focus	Evaluation criteria	Strategic data	Methods to collect data

Next, you will need to decide whether you want to transfer the table into a visual chain (e.g. using a flow diagram technique), so that the logic chain is visible and shared by other stakeholders.

Once agreed and shared, the material in the final column could be transferred into a scheduling tool such as a Gantt chart to operationalize and implement the evaluation framework.

Case study: Evaluating the impact of leadership coaching in a private sector partnership (adapting evaluation to respond to the conflicting priorities of the executive)

Snapshot

Sector: Private, national firm of general practitioner surveyors.
Governance: Board of equity partners (30).
Strategic focus: Primary goal for profit. Subordinate strategies for talent development and modernization (organizational overhaul).
Culture: Traditional partnership values of 'know, trust and respect'. Partners equally divided between 'custodian' (the future health of the business) and 'broker' (focus on short-term profit) mentalities. Partners are required to retire at 60.
Brand: Challenger.
Evaluation focus: Stakeholders with conflicting evaluation priorities

Context

This case study represents the experiences of a collaborative evaluation process within a private sector, multidisciplined national firm of general practice surveyors. The organization describes itself as 'an old fashioned' partnership, run by 30 equity partners, all of whom, in theory, have an equal stake in the business and its governance. The organization prides itself on a form of self-governance, built on the informal principles of 'know, trust and respect' and, although entry to the equity level of partnership is primarily predicated on outstanding financial performance, there is also a high degree of subjectivity over personal cultural fit, to be navigated by aspirant leaders.

The strategic focus for leadership and coaching: high potential talent and modernization

The organization has no formal HR department and, as with all other operational tasks, individual partners are delegated responsibility for various operational functions (to which they are neither qualified, nor always best suited). The idea that operational functions are in the hands of strategically minded partners means the organization tends to embark on formal operational projects in an informal manner. Accordingly, leadership development strategies have historically been unstructured and inconsistent, often on a 'do as I do' basis. More recently, coinciding with the appointment of a new senior partner from outside the organization, and the natural retirement cycle of an influential cadre of equity partners (required to retire at 60), leadership development has been highlighted to deliver a strategy for talent (for high performance through competitive differentiation), as part of a wider agenda for modernization.

It was clear from our interviews that the internal context was inherent, handed down from partner to partner, and in order to modernize, the organization would be challenged to manage numerous, ingrained cultural sensitivities and prejudices. This created a tension for the firm and its leadership: a traditional 'old fashioned' partnership structure, challenging itself to accommodate the unfamiliar values and beliefs of the new generation of diverse talent it was strategically targeting. This tension provided an entry point for coaching, as the organization responded to this challenge by hiring us, in the first instance, to provide executive coaching for its intake of graduates, interns and apprentices, as an alternative to the usual induction training it (and its competitors) usually provided.

The idiosyncrasies of partnership governance

At the heart of these cultural sensitivities, the organization's equity partners were divided equally between so-called 'custodians' and 'brokers' (the reader will remember that we introduced the characteristics of this organization in Chapter 3, as the third of our mini case studies, specifically to illustrate the evaluation paradox – evaluation metrics conflict with valued outcomes). In essence, the main distinction of a partnership is that the partners own the business and with that comes a culture of unconditional respect across the board. This form of governance is accepting of the different attitudes and motives of partners, between those focused on the future health of the business and its preservation, and those who see no further than bottom-line profit. Although there is no obvious judgement on either side, this form of governance does create inconsistencies and tensions down the line. This also translates to different departments, with some focused on outright wealth creation, while others provide a less profitable professional service. However, on the face of it, the organization recognizes the value of both as part of its position in the sector as a general practice.

In addition to the equity partners, the firm's leadership hierarchy comprises salaried partners and associates, all of whom have access to leadership coaching as part of the new leadership strategy, at varying levels. This new leadership strategy divided opinion (albeit surreptitiously) in line with the distinct attitudes of the two types of partner, where one school of thought (brokers) were found to be cynical about the benefits and impact of coaching, preferring the old-style development approach of do-as-I-do. However, those who promoted coaching saw this cynicism as a driving force for evaluation, as a convenient mechanism to convince the doubters and move forward the wider agenda for modernization.

The collaborative experience: uncovering the context for evaluation

The Jamieson Partnership has provided coaching programmes to the organization since 2016. The scope of coaching is expansive, ranging from executive graduate coaching to individual leadership coaching at equity partner level with, in between, various programmes for candidates within the leadership hierarchy. Accordingly, a strong professional relationship, albeit with 'custodians' of the business, has already been established, and the invitation to work in collaboration to design an evaluation system, primarily for the benefit of the organization but subsequently for inclusion in this book, was welcomed.

The first meeting

The collaborative process began with an initial meeting between Mark (as the coach evaluator), the senior partner and the partner with responsibility for talent management (the evaluation team). In the absence of an HR department, the focus for talent management becomes an interesting instinctive hybrid: neither wholly strategic nor operational. This means that the organization embraces coaching as a development strategy but, at the same time, is vague about coaching methods and outcomes, relegating it to the status of: *'We know it adds something, but not what that "something" is.'*

Coaching is provided across the leadership spectrum and it was decided to use a single leader at salaried partner level (in position to succeed as part of the next generation of equity partners) as the focus for our evaluation system. The evaluation team sat for an hour as part of an initial fact-finding process, investigating current evaluation attitudes, drivers, barriers and motivations. The meeting was quite informal and conversational (to set the tone for our collaborative relationship), with prompts for evaluation topics, rather than specific questions, embedded in a wider, coaching agenda. It was felt this preliminary meeting would not need to be replicated once an evaluation system was fully up and running.

This initial meeting provided interesting insights into the internal context, which also confirmed for us that evaluation was a potential gateway to inform wider strategic thinking. The prompts we used centred on the four problem areas emerging from our original research: data usage, dissemination, timelines and competency. The responses from this meeting provided a useful snapshot for the current state of evaluation and the perceived implications.

On data usage

There was no formal system to purposefully retrieve evaluation data. However, the idea of data usage was very one-dimensionally focused on financial compensation, closely aligned to the bottom-line profit of the business. Although all equity partners were entitled to take an equal share in the profits, there was apparent competition between departments about the contribution each makes. This, in part, was attributed to the alpha-male brokerage mentality of the industry as a whole which, it was acknowledged, potentially undermined the spirit of the partnership code. This sense of implicit competition placed a subtle pressure on the organization to focus on short-term performance, meaning that the way it viewed its leadership outcomes, was, in reality, far from equitable.

On dissemination

Due to the traditional partnership approach where so-called operational tasks are delegated among partners, dissemination of evaluation data was not considered a problem. Furthermore, the fact that each head of department had responsibility for their own teams seemed to be a perfectly logical chain of command for disseminating data. However, this was also an entry point for the bias and subjectivity that reflected the characters of different types of partner, and the organization had received feedback from some associates that career paths seemed dependent on which department they worked in and who their boss was.

On timelines

The organization prided itself on its retention rates which it used as evidence for a culture of which it was proud, enabling it to compete for top talent with its more illustrious competitors. However, as with dissemination, the organization could be accused of complacency as it was also retaining mediocre partners who were blocking the career path of up-and-coming stars, creating inconsistent timelines for promotion and hindering the organization's ability to accelerate top talent to leadership positions.

On competency

The fact that the organization was split between custodians and brokers meant that levels of competency to retrieve and disseminate evaluation data was mixed. The coaching cynics among the partners were unable to recognize that the generation below wanted and expected professional development as part of their package. Accordingly, those charged with evaluation often under-played or underestimated the impact of the coaching. Perhaps we should not be surprised that those partners not interested in coaching were less engaged with its measurement, and this influenced their competency to evaluate. This can be, in part, attributed to the idiosyncratic nature of the partnership governance, likened to an unwritten constitution – reliant on individual integrity, judgement and interpretation, where, if you're not truly engaged in an idea, but it is a part of your job (you could probably do without), competency becomes a problem.

From this initial meeting, the following Table (19) was produced by us, and for us, as an assessment for the environment for evaluation (we considered this a

Table 19   The context for evaluation (the evaluation environment)

Problem area	Evaluation lever	Emergent dimension of problem	Ambidextrous leadership and coaching focus
Data usage	Primary goals Organizational context	One-dimensionally focused on reward and recognition short-term Performance management	Performance versus future competitive relevance
Dissemination	Evaluation status Organizational context Multigenerational leadership pools	Inconsistent dissemination Frustrations of next leadership cohort	Efficiency savings versus talent management for high pivotal roles
Timelines	Primary goal Multigenerational leadership pools	Retention of high potentials Clear career paths Succession Cultural change	Performance versus future competitive relevance Management versus leadership Budgetary justification versus culture of collective understanding
Competency	Organizational context	Subjective judgment Bias Unconnected to the coaching culture Non-accountability Disinterest	Management versus leadership Coaching efficacy versus fuller range of coaching outcomes

useful reference point for our work but not deemed necessary for wider circulation to the evaluation team). The final column 'Ambidextrous leadership and coaching focus' was completed by the coach evaluator, primarily to assist the coaching focus, but also to form the basis of a framework (Table 20) to be shared with the evaluation team, illuminating the challenges for their organization's leadership in terms of a simple and relatable either-or decision-making context.

At this early stage we were interested to find how evaluation was already beginning to open up a wider strategic debate for the organization, simultaneously exposing a high level of complacency, operationally and attitudinally. For example, in the category for 'dissemination' a potential blind spot is clearly flagged, where previously the organization was blissfully unaware of the implications of inconsistency resulting from partner attitudes, which are now revealed to undermine the overarching talent strategy. Similarly, timelines when examined in this way pose a question about high retention levels, presumed to be positive, but when placed in the context of successful promotions as part of a longer-term outcome expose possible faultlines in succession strategy. Finally, the last column in the table starts to provide new strategic insights into the leadership role, providing precise areas for individual development, for future discussion.

The design experience

Having formulated the organizational context for evaluation (Table 19), we had a good idea of how receptive, or otherwise, it would be to our process, and what we needed to do to make it work. At this stage, we were able to apply our levers to examine the six challenges to evaluation in their unique organizational form (Table 20). These challenges are reimagined in the table (column 2) in the guise of leadership development pressure points emerging from the unique internal context. Through this process, we are able to introduce the notion of future evaluation targets.

Table 20 is the result of directly aligning emergent leadership outcome coaching targets and evaluation in the one place. In essence, the questions we had previously asked about evaluation had opened up a purview of leadership for us (and the client), including current challenges that defined the leadership character of the organization, and would help us produce data in the future (as part of the evaluation process) to inform the wider strategy. In Table 20, we (as the evaluator) collated this data for presentation to the evaluation team.

The second meeting

Table 20 was presented to the evaluation team at our second meeting. In the past, this time would have been allocated to a pre-programme briefing to discuss coaching outcomes. These previous meetings were informal, in line with the tone of the existing relationship between coach and client, but also, due to the lack of focus hitherto, on specific leadership outcomes. In other words, the organization was not quite sure what it wanted to achieve from the process; it just knew it was beneficial in some form or other. This particular meeting (our second) was scheduled to last an hour, and the agenda set out to discuss coaching outcomes and their alignment to the overarching strategy (talent management and modernization) for the primary goal (profit).

The table is our reading of the information from the first meeting (Table 19) and our extant knowledge of the organization, as seen through a lens of challenges and levers. In this case study, the second column contains our resultant assumptions about possible outcomes (challenges reimagined), and the explicit purpose of this meeting was to confirm or adjust these outcomes to connect with current strategies, to the satisfaction of the client. The iteration of Table 20 (below) includes minor adjustments made.

Table 20   Applying evaluation levers to unique challenges (emerging from Table 19 in the guise of insights for coaching) for coaching focus and evaluation targets, to create an ambidextrous framework (to inform the second meeting with the evaluation team)

Unique evaluation challenges	Dimensions and insights for leadership coaching	Influential levers	Ambidextrous dimensions for evaluation targets
Evaluation environment	Managing the tension between short-term financial goals for profit and long-term strategies for the future health of the firm Maintaining a partnership culture of collective understanding	Primary goal Organizational context	Balanced leadership behaviours Strategic mindset (long-term) 'Good Citizen'
Bias and contradiction	Retaining high potentials (providing a clear career path and consistent reward and recognition judgements across departments)	Organizational context Multigenerational leadership pools	Leadership over management Succession planning 'Global' vision Cross-selling strategies
Responsibility	Strategic goal setting The role of partner	Organizational context	New initiatives
Quality of data	Mentoring skills Strategic alignment	Multigenerational leadership pools Evaluation status	Management skills Mentoring targets
Generational reach	Coaching behaviours (for team management) Communication	Multigenerational organizational context	Retention and promotion data
Timelines (expectation)	Talent strategies	Multigenerational organizational context	Talent progress Ongoing projects

This table is a working ambidextrous framework, strategically aligned to the unique requirements of the client, which will allow us to identify blind spots and highlight areas for coaching and relevant targets for evaluation. For instance, in 'Bias and contradiction', the suggested dimension for coaching focuses on leadership behaviours that recognize the value of retaining high potential talent. In turn, these are now connected to evaluation targets that highlight coaching foci and are broken down into legitimate targets as part of ambidextrous dimensions. Here, a possible preoccupation with individual financial self-interest is refocused on 'global' strategies (such as talent development and cross-selling services) and included as key evaluation targets for both the coach and the leader. Similarly, where 'Responsibility' is seen as a challenge to evaluation, coaching outcomes for strategic goal setting and the role of the partner widens the evaluation criteria to incentivize the leader to focus on new initiatives.

Furthermore, in the categories of 'Generational reach' and 'Timelines', we can see how the framework begins to work as an ambidextrous tool, introducing intangible outcomes in the context of strategies for a primary goal. These sections justify and explain the role of the leader, and the expectations of the organization. As a tool for shaping leadership strategy, the emphasis of the framework (in this case) was deliberately weighted towards intangible outcomes, both for coaching and evaluation targets, and away from the one-dimensional broker mentality, which is where the partnership was perceived to be under pressure, and the main source of broader problems such as inconsistency, retention and succession. In applying ambidexterity to the evaluation process, we begin to see how resultant data has the potential to inform the wider strategy.

Where the evaluation model might sit

As part of the agenda for the second meeting of the evaluation team, we discussed the functionality of an evaluation model, specifically where it might fit. Having examined existing ambidextrous frameworks in place, to see if they could be adapted, we knew that the current leadership appraisal system was limited to a blanket one-size-fits-all approach, whereas our requirement was for an agile model that accepted the unique coaching requirements of the individual leader. Accordingly, it was decided to position the eventual evaluation framework alongside annual appraisals (at the end of the financial year), but as a separate entity. This distinction would be achieved through separate meetings between the sponsor, coach and the leader at the beginning (to agree outcomes) and at the end (to assess impact) of the programme, using a version of Table 20.

Producing an inventory of needs

Away from the evaluation team, we produced an inventory of needs to unlock a workable evaluation system. Using evaluation levers, specific blind spots emerged, which we converted to a unique set of organizational needs for a practical model.

Table 21   Using evaluation levers to uncover unique organizational blind spots (from Table 19) in the design of an evaluation framework

Evaluation lever	Definition	Blind spot	Inventory of needs
Primary goal	Financial performance for profit	Short-term focus on profit	Legitimization: long-term strategic
Evaluation status	Informal	Inconsistent subjective judgements from partners with different motives	Undistorted data
Multigenerational	Retention of leadership talent Succession Diversity in a traditional culture	Clear and consistent career paths	Non-financial incentives Consistent timelines for multidisciplines
Organizational context	'Old fashioned' partnership	Distinct 'custodian and broker' partners running the business Inherent attitudes and values undermining modernizing strategies	Consistent judgements across the partnership Not one-size-fits-all

This inventory of needs signposted the dimensions of our evaluation model, which we did not feel we needed to share with the evaluation team. At this stage we made a conscious decision to ration our access to the organization, in the knowledge that they did have other goals to pursue. We aimed to achieve a balanced relationship that earned their trust and allowed us intimate glimpses into the internal context and the overarching strategy, but did not prove bothersome to our (organizational) colleagues.

The evaluation experience

Stage 1: Arriving at evaluation criteria for the individual leader

As previously agreed, we chose a salaried partner as a guinea pig for our model. In this particular example, the leader has agreed coaching outcomes arising from her annual appraisal, including developing her team and high performance. High performance was broken down into delivery of short-term financial targets and longer-term initiatives, to reimagine her department's future post-Covid. Accordingly, the coach's focus was on the development of a strategic mindset, creative thinking, and a balanced approach to short- and long-term demands. At the initial meeting to discuss outcomes, the managing partner attended in his capacity as head of department.

Following on from this meeting, we (the coach evaluator) drew up the following framework (Table 22) as a road map for evaluation, to be shared with the sponsor at the end of the programme. The framework connects explorative and exploitative strategies for a primary goal and places them in the context of the individual leader's coaching needs (focus). In doing so, it produces a logical set of evaluation criteria.

Table 22   Evaluation framework for Partner A

Subordinate strategy for primary goal	Exploitative leadership targets	Explorative leadership targets	Leadership coaching focus	Evaluation criteria	Strategic data
Talent management	Recruitment, retention, succession	Motivating, inspiring, promoting	Coaching behaviours Social intelligence Communication	Promotion and retention Ambassador for recruitment Mentoring	
Short-term targets for profit	Allocating talent to high-impact positions	Unlocking discretionary energy of team	Ambidextrous balance	Departmental performance Organizational performance Management skills	
Long-term strategy for department post-Covid	Identifying opportunities	Creating a space to nurture new ideas	Strategic mindset Creative mindset Ambidextrous balance	Balanced approach to strategy New initiatives	

The framework provides evaluation criteria for which the organization was asked to produce corresponding leadership impact points. The strategic data column remains blank at this stage.

Stage 2: Monetizing impact and collecting strategic data

Table 23 Getting to financial and strategic values for coaching: template with leadership impact points selected by sponsor

Coaching investment	Leadership impact points	Estimated value	Strategic data
£10,000	**Talent management:** Promotions to partner Outstanding performers Recruitment initiatives		
	Short-term targets for profit: Performance of team and individual contributions		
	Long-term strategy for department post-Covid: Contribution to wider strategy		

Impact points provide a strategic context for leadership coaching outcomes and a financial reference point for their impact. Having produced these, the organization was then asked to provide an estimate of the value to the business of each impact point and an estimate of impact of coaching (see Figure 11). To achieve this, we used a simple percentage formula based on deadweight and attribution judgements (see Figure 12), ranging from 1 per cent (would have happened anyway) to 100 per cent (would not have happened at all). These figures are focused on return on investment: for every pound spent on coaching, what was the perceived value to the organization and the estimated percentage attributed to the impact of coaching (based on the unique development needs of the individual leader)? We asked the organization to make a judgement on the value of each impact point on an RoI basis:

Figure 11: Impact points broken down and weighted for monetization

Impact points	Estimated value and %
• Value to the organization of a new partner (salaried)	£25,000 @ 25%: £6,250
• Value to the organization of improved performance of independent team members	£100,000 @ 25%: £25,000
• Value to the organization of high potential recruitment	£50,000 @ 20%: £10,000
• Value to the organization of new initiatives	None (in the pipeline)

Figure 12: Final evaluation framework for Partner A showing RoI

Investment	Impact points	Additional value	Attributable-deadweight calculator	Net added value
£10,000	Value to the organization of a new partner (salaried)	£25,000	25%	£6,250
	Value to the organization of improved performance of independent team members	£100,000	25%	£25,000
	Value to the organization of high potential recruitment	£50,000	20%	£10,000
	Value to the organization of new initiatives	None	Nil	Nil
				−£10,000
Total RoI				**£31,250**

All impact points have been framed as tangible (exploitative) outcomes but can be traced back to their explorative contributory factors in Table 22 (notice we have excluded straightforward financial performance targets from these calculations as a way of further distancing ourselves from a one-dimensional evaluation approach focused on short-term profit). The process and the subsequent accuracy of the estimated sums were discussed by the evaluation team. It was felt that these were necessarily a judgement call and there might be some distortion through subjectivity or inconsistency. The reader would be justified in pointing out that any system reliant on the subjective, often tendentious, judgements of different partner personalities takes the organization back to square one. However, this model is designed to expose inconsistency and provide a clear and unambiguous understanding of outcomes, impact and financial value, where any overt inconsistency can be brought into question. Furthermore, the organization felt it was their place (quite rightly) to make these judgements because they had knowledge of worth (to the organization), the individual leaders (everyday experience of their development needs), and outcomes (the type of leaders they wanted to develop).

In this case study, an estimated financial value of £31,250 was assigned to the original coaching investment for this partner, representing an estimated return of 312.5 per cent.

Stage 3: Strategic data: informing the wider strategy

One of our key observations about the collaborative process is when to leave well alone. There are certain areas of the organization that will always remain closed to the external consultant, however strong and trusting is the collaborative relationship. The role of the collaborative coach evaluator is to guide, make recommendations and arbitrate when called upon. The coach evaluator should not presume to try to influence decisions relating to worth, individual leaders or desired [leadership] outcomes. Similarly, when it comes to strategic data, the collaborator coach can only really help produce frameworks that connect data resulting from the evaluation of the impact of leadership coaching to given strategies and impact points. It is clearly for the organization to use this data as they see fit.

In this case study process, the collection of strategic data is formally introduced in Table 22, although the idea that evaluation data can inform the wider strategy is implanted at the very first meeting of the evaluation team. In Table 22, the strategic data column is left uncompleted as it is designed to be a work in progress, especially as this is a pilot programme, and it is envisaged that databanks will be most usefully built up over a number of years. However, we discussed the destination of strategic data and the organization produced the following hotspots:

Table 24 Strategic hotspots for evaluation data

Coaching investment	Leadership impact points	Estimated value	Strategic data (to inform)
£10,000	**Talent management:** Promotions to partner Outstanding performers Recruitment initiatives		Career paths (including succession strategy) Training and development policy Type of talent we should be recruiting Retention strategy
	Short-term targets for profit: Performance of team and individual contributions		Reward and recognition policy Non-financial incentivization
	Long-term strategy for department post-Covid: Contribution to wider strategy		New workplace environment initiative Well-being and mental health policy New strategic initiatives: opportunities and threats

These hotspots do not have the benefit of a well-established evaluation system from which to evolve; however, the organization assured us that they were relevant and useful, and more than sufficient incentive to develop this aspect of the evaluation system.

Final thoughts

The collaborative process was enabled by a strong existing professional relationship built over the last five years. Therefore, this case cannot be considered a typical examination of the coach–client relationship as a potential stumbling block for the evaluation process. Regardless of the good relations with the organization, we would like to thank them, not just for their cooperation, but for the enthusiasm to work together on this project. The positive response to evaluation may also be partly explained by its coincidence with the current leadership challenges facing the organization to modernize.

Despite the energetic cooperation of the organization, we made every attempt to limit their exposure to the mechanics of evaluation design, assuming a limited attention span. In total, the evaluation team met twice for a total of 2 hours (see Figure 13 flow chart). The feedback we received on the necessary deliberations to complete Table 23 suggested that this was a short and focused process due to the identification of impact points simplifying (and making tangible) outcomes.

One of the emerging questions for future research was whether the model would be easily transferable more widely across the leadership hierarchy, specifically at associate level, where coaching tended to be more generic, focused on groups. We will also be interested to learn, over time, the part our evaluation system played in helping the organization to achieve its agenda to modernize, specifically in negating the source of bias and contradiction from the internal context.

As a private sector firm focused on a primary goal for profit, the visual design of this particular evaluation framework was influenced by the organization's familiarity with accountancy spread sheets. Although it is no criticism, it is interesting to recall the words of Maslow (1998), which still clearly endure today, encapsulating the challenge of leadership development:

Accountants must try to figure out some way of turning into balance sheet terms the intangible personnel values that come from improving the people of the organisation.

Hopefully, we have gone some way to achieving this.

Evaluation flowchart

Figure 13: Evaluation process flowchart

1. First meeting with client (evaluation team). Wider discussion around coaching outcomes and examination of the internal context to understand the environment for evaluation. **1 hour – all**

2. Production of **Table 1** by coach for evaluator reference and early indications of coaching foci. **1 hour – coach evaluator**

3. Application of evaluation levers to six general challenges to evaluation **(Table 2)**. Compiled by coach evaluator for presentation to the evaluation team. **1 hour – coach evaluator**

4. Second meeting of evaluation team to discuss **Table 2** and positioning of evaluation system in the strategic chain. **1 hour – all**

5. Producing an inventory of needs **(Table 3)** to reveal and record evaluation blind spots. For evaluator use. **1 hour – coach evaluator**

6. Individual leader meeting with leadership candidate, coach and managing partner to agree strategically aligned outcomes and development areas **(Table 4)**. **1 hour – coach and leadership candidate**

7. Individual leader meeting with coach to assess impact of coaching to be discussed formally at leader's appraisal. **1 hour – coach and leadership candidate**

8. Selection of appropriate leadership impact points, their value and weighting **(Table 5)** by sponsor. **Unspecified – sponsor stakeholder**

9. Completion of final evaluation framework **(Figure 2)**. **Unspecified – Sponsor**

10. Retrieval and dissemination of strategic data. **Ongoing – organization**

Estimated time spent on evaluation

- Evaluation team – 2 hours.
- Coach evaluator (including attendance at evaluation team meetings, and additional one-to-one objectives and assessment sessions which were charged) – 7 hours.
- Leadership candidate (coachee) – 2 hours (excluding internal appraisals).
- Sponsor/stakeholder/department head – unspecified.

Case study: Evaluating the impact of leadership coaching in the third sector (achieving behavioural return on investment)

Snapshot

Sector: Third sector, national youth charity.
Governance: Board of trustees and operational executive.
Strategic focus: Primary goal to end youth poverty within a generation. Subordinate strategy: aligning vision and accountability targets through a single operating model.
Culture: Servant-hearted leadership; psychologically informed environment.
Brand: Market leader.
Evaluation focus: A charity run as a business: how to achieve behavioural RoI.

Context and background

In 2017, we carried out global research for the EMCC (Wall et al. 2017) on the attitudes of coaches to evaluation. Our work uncovered some interesting themes, suggesting that approaches to evaluation broadly reflected the commercial mindsets and competitiveness of the country in question. For instance, at one extreme, in the USA, leadership coaching evaluation was dominated by the need to prove a precise (often improbable) RoI, while at the other end of the spectrum, in less commercially aggressive or developed countries (Eastern Europe), coaching was at a comparatively nascent stage and evaluation hardly registered.

This knowledge explained a lot about the diversity of evaluation attitudes, reinforcing our assertion that, for coaching (and evaluation), a one-size-fits-all approach is unworkable and strategically random. Accordingly, we used these insights from the EMCC research to make parallel comparisons with the different sectors with whom we were working (solely in the UK) to develop the notion, posited earlier in this book, that different sectors imagine evaluation in different ways, reflecting the unique needs and primary goals of the individual organization. In other words, we were able to anticipate sector attitudes to evaluation purely on the basis of their commercial or purposive focus. As a start point to our work with an organization this was very useful; however, it also opened our eyes to the importance of system transferability and built-in flexibility, emphasizing the relevance of our research across different sectors for this book.

As with geographic distinctions, different sectors, similarly, represent clusters of multispeed attitudes to leadership, coaching and evaluation, mirroring the commercial focus (normally the primary goal) of the organization. In this case study, we relate our experiences of designing an evaluation system for a national youth charity, where the primary goal for purpose put a new and different complexion on leadership outcomes and ambidextrous dimensions for us to consider as we went about our task. In this context, leaders were found to have both technical and motivational coaching needs, reflecting the ambidextrous characteristics of third sector organizations, which in this case were: short-term financial targets for accountability, versus long-term visionary goals to eradicate youth poverty in the UK. Working with the organization's senior leadership, we found financial pressures for accountability were just as intense as those in the private sector, the main difference being that leaders in the third sector had neither the expertise nor the motivation (incentivized by purpose rather than financial self-interest), to cope with unexplained short-term targets. Articulated by the CEO in an earlier interview:

> People do not join us for the money. They've come here because they want to do something good for someone else – and get paid something.

Therefore, as coaches, we were challenged to deliver highly focused commercial interventions to a leadership cohort who had no interest in financial management, swerving monetary targets in pursuit of a leadership career unerringly focused on good deeds.

Within this context, the organization had a steep and multilayered leadership hierarchical structure. However, despite many levels of formally recognized leadership, coaching was non-discriminatory (all managers at all levels had access to the same coaching programme), and leadership functioned as a quasi-cooperative society where, in theory at least, all members were treated equally. At the heart of the leadership culture, leaders were described as 'servant-hearted'.

This style of leadership was formally endorsed in 2018, when the organization transitioned to a psychologically informed environment (PIE – regularly adopted by the third sector since 2010) focused on functioning in a way that considered the emotional and psychological needs of both staff and 'clients' (people who are in, or who have experienced, poverty).

In 2020, we were invited to advise on a new leadership programme, on the basis that management was struggling to deliver the hard targets influenced by government funding and donor demands, while being focused on a soft primary goal for purpose. The organization was alerted to this potential flaw in its leadership development by a high rate of attrition and low leadership morale.

Accordingly, the coaching programme we proposed accommodated the unique ambidextrous characteristics of the organization, setting out to prove tangible targets and intangible goals were not necessarily mutually exclusive. Our coaching model was built around a Level 5 leader development programme (Collins 2005): an ambidextrous approach reflecting the organization's values in tandem with a pressing need to operate at the highest level of performance. Level 5 leadership is not a new concept and has been attributed to high achieving organizations since 2001. Described as 'the triumph of humility and fierce resolve' (Collins 2005), we felt it was an appropriate approach to leadership coaching, given the unique ambidextrous context set within a psychologically informed environment. Our aim was to bring to life the concept of servant-hearted leadership in terms that could not only be understood and implemented, but subsequently evaluated.

Unlike the previous case study, the organization was not at all cynical about the benefits of leadership development; if anything, it could be argued, it was too undiscriminating, therefore un-targeted and non-specific. This positive attitude to leadership coaching removed a significant barrier to evaluation; however, the current approach (to evaluation) was narrow and one-dimensional, unaligned to the overarching leadership strategy, reluctantly focused on financial accountability.

Influenced by external stakeholders (government, local authorities and donors), this singular focus was at odds with leaders' motivation and the organization's primary goal, emphasizing the areas of least interest to leadership and simultaneously, strategically limited in terms of a critical primary goal. Therefore, the context into which we stepped was an organization promoting a free-for-all leadership community, espousing an intangible, ambiguous style of leadership (and development) to achieve an explorative but highly impactful primary goal, while focusing evaluation on someone else's short-term financial targets of little strategic importance.

The eagle-eyed reader will recognize this organization from Chapter 2 (Case study 2), exemplifying the use of a conceptual balance mechanism (a single operating model).

The collaborative experience: uncovering the context for evaluation

The Jamieson Partnership was introduced to the organization in 2015 and has provided one-to-one coaching for leaders at all levels. During that time, the organization had rolled out a separate, general development programme (the Leadership Journey) across the leadership hierarchy, aligned to a corresponding existing leader behavioural framework espousing the values of the charity. This programme was designed and delivered by an established (with the organization) provider; scheduled for review after 12 months by an internal Strategy Delivery Group, collating data from pulse survey feedback from those leaders having taken part.

The review process was conceived to better understand the development needs of organizational leaders, to inform future programmes and identify priority leadership skills. What it ended up doing was widening the gap between espoused leadership values and behaviours, and organizational business imperatives. In essence, leaders were found to be confused by contradictions in the system, specifically a set of values that were practically ambiguous and open to multiple interpretations, seemingly at odds with the short-term financial targets upon which they were being judged. Leadership development was in conflict with the tasks leaders were required to perform (soft skills for hard targets) and, consequently, the values the organization proudly stood by were not being brought to life by the current programme, meaning they were either misunderstood or, worse still, dismissed cynically as rhetoric. The bottom line from these reviews was that leaders were found to be demoralized and retention of leadership talent continued to challenge the organization.

Our existing relationship with the organization, and an invitation to provide an external review of the Leadership Journey, formed the basis of our collaborative relationship. Initially, an informal meeting was convened between Mark (as the coach/consultant), the CEO and the director with responsibility for Learning and Development. It was clear from the organization's own feedback that the current programme, despite being designed around the organization's stated values and the psychologically informed environment within which it operated, was missing the target, specifically in terms of supporting and developing leadership. Acting as consultants, we provided a review as well as an alternative proposal, which included an evaluation of impact framework.

The evaluation focus was an important and highly relevant part of our proposition, as our review would go on to highlight:

a The current programme had no financial evaluation element at a time when the organization was particularly sensitive to budgetary accountability.

b Assessment data was retrieved from first-hand experiences and limited to future programme design.

c The organization needed a (balance) mechanism (an evaluation framework) to disambiguate and explain ambidextrous leadership tasks by refocusing them on the organization's primary goal, to counter the evident disconnect between hard targets and soft goals resulting from the internal context (PIE).

In addition, we also found divisions in the senior executive team (SET) over the suitability of a commercially focused executive coaching programme in a values driven organization. This mindset highlighted the confused personality of the organization that defined its unique ambidextrous character, placing the onus on us to provide evidence that exploitative and explorative targets could work in harmony for the greater good – something we intended to do through an integrated evaluation framework.

Having weighed up what we already knew about the organization's internal context and the emphasis on behavioural outcomes aligned to a set of values, we designed a coaching programme focused on delivering Level 5 leadership (Figure 14).

Figure 14: Level 5 leader framework and coaching dimensions

Leadership level	Coaching dimensions
Level 1 – Highly capable individual	Professional competence and organizational mindset (awareness of the overarching strategy and primary goal)
Level 2 – Team player	Using skills, experience and expertise to achieve team goals
Level 3 – Highly competent manager	Executive development for operational and managerial efficiency and effectiveness
Level 4 – Team leader	Leadership coaching to meet performance and behavioural expectations, and achieve primary goal
Level 5 – Organizational leader	Balanced leadership (judgement) The proven abilities for Levels 1–4 in alignment with organizational values

Defining the unique ambidextrous character

We believed that this approach accommodated the unique ambidextrous context of the organization, developing and supporting leaders to close the gap between idealism and implementation: negating contradictions and rationalizing the tension between business imperatives (outcomes for survival) and personal leadership motivations (vision for real change). In the first instance, we used this gap as a reference point to crystallize the organization's unique definition of ambidexterity: to manage the tension between exploitative and explorative goals, exacerbated by personal and professional motivations, minimal financial compensation and seemingly strategically unaligned to the primary goal – ending youth poverty.

The first meeting

Although we had previously met as a collaborative team to review the Leadership Journey programme, it was our subsequent meeting that we have designated as the first in this evaluation process. At this meeting, we unveiled our Level 5 leader framework as a road map for coaching, to deliver leadership capable of executing the tenets of top-level management while simultaneously working to the organization's values. It was the boldness of our statement of intent that provided the entry point for evaluation of impact, moving it up the agenda from an add-on to a facilitator of leadership strategy. The inclusion of an integrated evaluation framework supported our proposal, acting as a focal point to link accountability and vision. Emphasizing evaluation also highlighted the fact that it was currently conspicuous by its absence and, contrastingly, the confidence we had in our coaching proposal (to prove it worked).

Having established the unique ambidextrous character of the organization, provided a suitable coaching response and introduced the idea of evaluation as a key strategic facilitator, we set about completing the picture of what the context for evaluation looked like, using our four evaluation problematics. Below are some of the indicative results from our preliminary fact-finding meeting with the (evaluation) team.

On data usage

Currently, the charity does not evaluate for data as such. The closest it gets to evaluation is to carry out a review process of the Leadership Journey programme as part of their operational best practice. All this reveals is whether those receiving the coaching feel they are getting benefit, and what might need to be considered in any future programme. There is recognition that it should do better with evaluation in terms of proving financial accountability to its donors and funders, where there is a perception that funds go directly to supporting a young person. Rightly or wrongly, these funding sources are attracted by headline destinations: a building; a project, etc, and contributing to a leadership development budget for staff is not so appealing and requires justification. Therefore, the organization would welcome a system to provide some hard evidence of both the impact of leadership coaching and its overall connection to their vision.

On dissemination

As things stand, there is very little data to disseminate. However, what the organization does struggle with is getting buy-in, especially from middle managers, to targets that they cannot connect to the mission they are on– the reason they joined. The charity acknowledges that purpose can become easily disconnected from what people are doing in their day job and sees the distribution of data from evaluation as a possible route for leaders to find a way to reconcile targets to vision.

On timelines

Ideally, leadership outcomes are monitored through the destination of the young person: whether they are in settled accommodation, employment, training or education. And the organization is making attempts to do this by connecting the performance of its leaders directly to young people. However, this is necessarily a long-term assessment and it is difficult to keep track over a number of years; also, they are limited to applying a one-size-fits-all timeline to a very diverse and different group of people.

On competency

The organization's attitude is that it is very easy to measure data (assuming you have it); it is less easy to measure behavioural change. Here, the implication is that they do not have the right data and are therefore measuring the wrong things. In other words, by their own admission, they neither have the data nor the targets for measurement.

Resulting from this initial meeting, and the application of evaluation levers to the four problem areas, we were able to produce Table 25 as a sketch of the environment for evaluation. As with the previous case study, this table was for our own reference (not circulated); however, the unique ambidextrous characteristics in the final column would form the basis for future discussions over the leadership challenges of operating in a psychologically informed environment.

Table 25 The context for evaluation (the evaluation environment)

Problem area	Evaluation lever	Emergent dimension of problem	Ambidextrous leadership and coaching focus
Data usage	Evaluation status	**Limited:** Informal* review system based on participant 'feel-good' and limited to future programme design **Non-financial:** Unspecified and untargeted	Short-term financial targets versus long-term vision Multiple stakeholders: high financial accountability versus headline funding destination Executive leadership coaching versus PIE Leadership Journey (programmes)
Dissemination	Multigenerational leadership pools Organizational context Primary goal	**Irrelevant and unrelatable:** Steep leadership hierarchy Lack of collective cultural buy-in Attrition and retention rates	Management versus leadership Performance versus purpose Non-financial incentives versus motivational compensation

(Continued)

Table 25 (Continued)

Problem area	Evaluation lever	Emergent dimension of problem	Ambidextrous leadership and coaching focus
Timelines	Primary goal	**Indeterminate:** Long-term outcome tracking	Remote leadership outcomes: job entry (attainment) versus career inspiration
		Not adaptable: Inconsistent due to mixed abilities and lack of isolation	Opportunity generation: job versus career
Competency	Primary goals	**Non-strategic:** irrelevant data and data destination	Financial responsibility versus long-term leadership development behaviours
	Evaluation status	Formal* via operational HR department focused on conventional HR targets in opposition to strategic intentions (strategic disconnect)	Operational versus strategic mindset

Initially, we were reluctant to include both informal and formal descriptions of evaluation status in this table, as it could be confusing to the reader. However, we felt it was important to include both definitions, to relate the complexity of the internal context rather than attempt to conveniently shoo-in one or the other. In this case study, evaluation status was technically formal, the domain of an operational HR department; at the same time, the approach to evaluation was nearly non-existent, akin to an informal status. It was felt that both these definitions characterized emergent evaluation problems for the organization, and warranted inclusion.

As with the first case study, this initial framework provided fascinating, previously unrecognized, insights into the internal context. We now had a clear sight of the unique challenges of leadership as well as a fore-glimpse of the potential for evaluation to contribute valuable information into the wider strategy, not to mention a practical view of the organizational landscape, into which our evaluation model would need to fit.

The design experience

One key distinction of this particular case study was that we were not parachuting in an evaluation system to an existing leadership coaching programme, but including it as part of a new proposal. This meant that the emphasis was not wholly on evaluation during our collaboration. It also allowed us to experience evaluation as part of an integrated coaching programme and examine whether this was a more convenient design process, unencumbered by an existing structure. As this was the case, it was relatively straightforward to build our framework connecting coaching outcomes to evaluation (Table 26) by applying

Table 26 Applying evaluation levers for leadership outcomes and coaching focus, and evaluation targets

Unique evaluation challenges	Dimension and insight for leadership coaching	Influential lever	Ambidextrous dimension for evaluation targets
Evaluation environment	Communication skills to create a culture of collective understanding	Primary goal Evaluation status	Promoting SOM: Departmental cross-selling and referrals
Bias and contradiction	Personal and professional development: aligning values (personal and organizational) with operational excellence	Multigenerational leadership pools	Retention and recruitment Team performance targets
Responsibility	Developing a balanced strategic mindset for operational targets as a subordinate strategy for a primary goal (identifying with targets and setting new goals)	Organizational context Evaluation status	Advanced delegation Team talent management: promotions and retention
Quality of data	Professional judgement and prioritization	Organizational context Evaluation status	Input into operational and strategic team and organizational targets
Generational reach	Communication, coaching behaviours and mentoring skills	Multigenerational leadership pools Organizational context	Time and capacity management
Timelines	Soft skills for inspiring and motivating for vital distinction between short-term targets for homeless young people in poverty achieved through systems management and life-changing sustainable goals	Primary goal	A 'safe' environment to foster creativity and long-term innovation Advanced communication skills to inspire

evaluation levers, despite the complex and layered characteristics of the ambidextrous context (short-term performance targets versus long-term mission; intense financial accountability versus non-financially motivated vocation; technical management for entry level jobs for young people versus inspirational leadership for long-term sustainable careers).

The second meeting

Table 26 formed the agenda for our second meeting. To produce this framework, we had to reorient our levers to reflect sector priorities to make them work for us. The primary goal lever remained focused on the main work of the organization, but its emphasis on purpose over profit meant that it was multidimensional and open to interpretation. On the plus side, this duality made it easier to apply and adapt to ambidextrous positions. Evaluation status was no longer a simple binary lever, but seen as a hybrid, accepting the worst traits of informal and formal approaches. Organizational context was similarly multilayered emphasizing unique ambidextrous challenges, while multigenerational leadership pools were connected to the steep leadership hierarchy, reflecting the conflict between leaders who identified with, and focused on, short-term targets, and more idealistic leaders who struggled to make sense of the organizational dichotomy as part of a vocational career choice (generally defined by either age or length of service). Here, our framework took on a new dimension, untangling the confusing and contradictory demands placed upon leaders, and, by making sense of these expectations, introducing an entirely new set of leadership outcomes. Unsurprisingly, having successfully unlocked the leadership conundrum for the organization, when we reconvened for our second meeting, evaluation was present but took a back seat to the wider leadership strategy. Despite this secondary position, the potentially rich vein of strategic data that might emanate from an effective evaluation system, illuminated for the first time by this table, was a lightbulb moment for the group.

Where the evaluation model might sit

Having expanded the strategic relevance of evaluation by facilitating a far-reaching discussion on leadership, it seemed apposite, at our second meeting, to explore where evaluation would be best placed to act as an effective pivot for both leadership and overarching strategy and, unlike the previous case study, there was a real opportunity to examine the possibility of expanding an existing ambidextrous framework.

Within the complex ambidextrous environment, the organization was working to a single operating model (SOM – see also Chapter 2, case study 2). The SOM set out to connect exploitative targets, seen as incompatible with the motives of leaders, to an explorative outcome, by creating a direct route for every job into the primary goal. However, it was not well disseminated or easily understood by lower levels of the leadership hierarchy. On closer examination the SOM, in its current form, was not a framework we felt could be easily expanded to include evaluation. We rejected this idea for two reasons: firstly, it was not being effectively implemented and therefore remained unproven; secondly, we had the rare luxury of being able to use our own leadership development model, where evaluation was integrated. However, we could see that, in theory, this was a useful ambidextrous framework at the heart of the organization's strategy, where evaluation could comfortably sit alongside. We also took into consideration the emphasis on leadership behaviours as a way to achieve high performance and the need to abide by the organization's proud code of values. Accordingly, we imagined our evaluation system fitting into the organization's strategy chain, thus:

Figure 15: Where evaluation might fit as a strategic pivot

```
S — Level 5 leader coaching — Behaviours          / Sub Strat.
O — Level 5 leader coaching — Behaviours — EVALUATION-Sub. Strat.— PG
M — Level 5 leader coaching — Behaviours          \ Sub. Strat.
```

Producing an inventory of needs

As a result of our first two meetings, our inventory of organizational needs for the practical design of our evaluation system looked like this:

Table 27 Putting evaluation levers to work to address organizational blind spots in the design of a workable system (not shared)

Evaluation lever	Definition	Blind spot (emerging from internal context)	Inventory of needs
Primary goal	Performance for purpose not for profit	High financial pressures set against non-financial incentives	Legitimization: understanding and buy-in to subordinate exploitative strategies for an explorative primary goal
Evaluation status	Hybrid: informal/ formal	Irrelevant and limited targets	Data: clearly identified relevant targets
Multigenerational	Steep leadership hierarchy Age and length of service	Communication for collective understanding Pragmatic versus idealistic attitudes	Disambiguation (communication and assessment)
Organizational context	Psychologically informed environment Servant-hearted leadership	Limited financial acumen Low moral	Consistent ambidextrous judgements to accommodate hard financial targets

The evaluation experience

Stage 1: Arriving at outcomes and evaluation criteria for the individual leader

This case study focuses on evaluation of impact of our version of Level 5 leader coaching on a department head in the organization. We should state that we have isolated the evaluation experience for the purposes of this book, whereas in real life this was part of a broader assessment of our pilot coaching programme (of which, evaluation was just one, albeit integral, part).

Unlike the previous case study, we expected this framework to translate smoothly across the leadership hierarchy due to the culture of leadership equality, the minimal impact of reward and recognition systems, and the capability of the programme to disambiguate ambidextrous outcomes (a key target for the organization). Table 28 reflects the agreed outcomes for the leader and accompanying coaching focus (resulting from an introductory one-to-one 'chemistry' session with the coach). The similarities with the previous case

Table 28 Evaluation framework for departmental head (middle manager)

Subordinate strategy for primary goal	Exploitative leadership targets	Explorative leadership targets	Leadership coaching focus	Evaluation criteria	Strategic data
Talent management	Retention of talent	Communicating, motivating and inspiring	Coach/ manager behaviours Communication	Retention and promotion data	
Team management for short-term targets for funding and accountability	Opportunity generation and operational excellence	Communicating the values, aims and goals of the organization for culture of collective understanding Team structuring and allocation of resources	Executive coaching Strategic thinking Communication	Departmental performance Commercial relationships Restructuring teams	
Long-term strategy for people experiencing poverty	Managing needs for a job and a home	Preparing for a career and permanent housing	Operational excellence inc. time and capacity management Creativity Strategic thinking	Ex-poverty short-term data (tba) Ex-poverty long-term (5 year) data (tba) Cross-selling and referrals (to other depts) data	

study around the subordinate strategies are purely coincidental (although it might be argued that these categories naturally emerge from an ambidextrous perspective and, therefore, will regularly appear throughout the process in one form or another), but also provide a useful compare and contrast opportunity. The strategic data column remains blank at this stage and merely functions as a prompt for future focus.

This table was designed to satisfy the inventory of needs (Table 27) emerging from the organizational internal context by building chains between ambidextrous (exploitative and explorative) outcomes in the context of the primary goal (*'Putting purpose back at the heart of people's roles'*). It recognizes that reconciling targets to purpose requires the organization to identify clear goals and remove the hybrid (informal–formal) status of evaluation, allowing for a formal process with explicit unambiguous outcomes, relevant and relatable for both assessment and dissemination. Finally, the model provides a clear road map for leadership to prioritize outcomes and form professional judgements that are consistent across the ambidextrous framework.

The third meeting

We presented this framework at our third meeting with the team, where it was positively received as clearly deconstructing hitherto complex and contradictory leadership expectations:

> *This is very useful. It captures what we need our leaders to do and gives us relevant targets to assess their and our progress.*

At this meeting, we became aware that our model naturally gravitated towards, and tracked, the three fundamental leadership goals of the organization: accountability, behaviours and long-term outcomes. This continued to reinforce our confidence that we were on the right track for an evaluation model that had the capacity to act as a strategic informant, as well as making sense of the leadership role and providing short-term financial accountability.

Stage 2: Monetizing impact for accountability, assessing behavioural change and collecting strategic data (for social return on investment)

These two quotations from the CEO encapsulated the evaluation character of the organization:

> *Bricks and mortar outcomes should be aligned to the leadership value framework. Our leaders' development is evaluated on how well they live the values to deliver hard tangible targets.*
>
> *So, we are not looking for RoI but behavioural RoI, expressed in better outcomes for the impoverished community.*

We took this to mean that the emphasis for our evaluation model would be on behavioural assessment for performance and strategic data. Therefore, unlike the previous case study in Chapter 7, where the organization sought a bank-balance calculation to evidence a financial return on investment, and strategic data to predict leadership outcomes in dynamic markets, this was to be a more complicated, nuanced relationship with evaluation.

Accordingly, we felt we had three major challenges to producing a workable and relevant evaluation system. Our first challenge was to understand how the organization visualized an evaluation system, so we could produce a model that spoke their language (attractive and therefore relatable). Due to the nature of its primary goal, the concept of evaluation had been dismissed, probably because of its connotations to financial outcomes, and rejected as not appropriate (beyond some limited accountability). Ironically, we found that the commercial pressure on those leaders working in the organization was on a par with the private sector, the main difference being that leaders in the third sector tend not to be financially motivated or competitive. This attitude was manifest as a single focus on leadership behaviours (as an acceptable bridge between targets and goals, and referred to as behavioural RoI by the CEO) as the deliverer of high performance, and this was our second challenge.

Behavioural RoI, to the best of our knowledge, does not exist, and we would need to adapt our final evaluation framework to include an appropriate calculation for the impact of our coaching programme, specifically on leadership behaviours and their influence on organizational outcomes. In considering this, we decided we would include three leader behavioural categories, in response to the inconsistent attitudes across a steep leadership hierarchy: Improved, Maintained, Excelled. It was anticipated that these categories would form a new version of the attributable-deadweight function in our final calculations.

Finally, we were also conscious of the social return on investment (SRoI), emerging as a focus from the subordinate strategies for the primary goal. These outcomes were all characterized by indeterminate timelines, subjective judgements, idiosyncratic personalities (mixed abilities and motivations) and logistical barriers for data collection. We discussed with the team various models to measure SRoI; however, it was felt that this was a separate, wider evaluation project, not directly connected to the impact of leadership coaching, but informed by data emerging from that process.

The framework (Table 28) was designed to be used in collaboration with the individual leader, as part of the appraisal process. At that meeting, along with outcomes, impact points would be agreed for evaluation. The strategic data column has been allocated to the wider overarching strategy to inform social return on investment and is incomplete at this stage.

How we identified impact points

This evaluation model reflects the requirements of the organization, emphasizing financial accountability and behavioural development. Impact points emerged from connecting the subordinate strategies to evaluation criteria in Table 28, subsequently developed and agreed with the leader. This version of the evaluation model (Table 29) directly connects coaching to value dimensions,

Table 29 Demonstrating impact and strategic and financial value

Agreed impact point	Coaching dimension	Demonstrable impact	Contribution to an organiza-tional target or a primary goal	Estimated value
Talent management: individual leadership development	What is your leadership brand? Finding your authentic leadership voice	Growing confidence as a leader in contribution to management meetings	Accelerate promotion of young leaders as part of succession strategy	Retention of talent: £7,500 (disruption, recruitment, bedding-in)
	Your impact as a leader on others	Contributed to organizational strategy conference as key note speaker	Retain talent	
	Developing your leadership EQ (emotional intelligence)	Member of training and development committee		
	Developing your leadership judgement			
Team management: team-leadership development	Communicating as a leader	Successful restructuring of team	Streamlining teams for efficiency and improved delivery of targets	Efficiency savings: £22,000
	Awareness of what other people need from you as a leader	Regular and dynamic team meetings	Improve retention stats	Improved performance of individual team members to achieve targets: £16,000
	Delegating to empower	Appraisals successfully carried out on all team members	Revisit and refresh people strategy	
	Difficult conversations			
	Developing your authoritative voice	Retention of all team members during transition	Improve accountability through effective deployment of talent and cost savings	

(Continued)

Table 29 (Continued)

Agreed impact point	Coaching dimension	Demonstrable impact	Contribution to an organizational target or a primary goal	Estimated value
Team management: delivery of team targets	Prioritizing goals	Revised short-term targets (team) achieved	Improve profitability	Year-on-year improvement on hitting team target: £20,000 (in new funding)
	Effective delegation		Maintain growth trajectory	
	Time management		Protect organization by delivering short-term targets	
	Performance management			
Long-term strategy: contribution to wider organizational strategy	Creative and innovative thinking	Review of current team strategy undertaken and delivered	Review organizational strategy for 2020	Team contribution to projected growth figures for 2021: £75,000
	Thinking beyond your team		Seek opportunities for expansion through new markets, collaborations and partnerships	
	Managing up	Effective contribution to higher management meetings		Team contribution to cross-selling organizational expertise: £25,000
	Strategic alignment		Attract best talent	
	Collaboration	Cross-dept. initiative proposed for marketing strategy		
	Networking			
Estimated value of impact				**£165,500**

partially as a result of evaluation being integral to the new Level 5 leader proposal, to maintain the focus on impact. The estimated values were provided by the (evaluation) team in collaboration with those directors with relevant departmental responsibility.

The reader should note how this table has evolved and adapted (in comparison to Table 23 in the previous chapter) to the organization's (and sector) primary goal focus. This version reflects a more complex multidimensional primary goal (as opposed to a singular focus on profit), and an emphasis on leadership behaviours. It is also distinct, being part of an integrated evaluation framework within a new coaching programme, rather than a shooed in system to fit an existing leadership development strategy. The final iteration (Table 30) rationalizes estimated added value, removing the organizational projected growth figure (£75,000 as not directly attributable to coaching) and applying the unique behavioural impact calculator (as a behaviourally focused alternative to the attributable-deadweight reckoner).

You will recall, as part of our efforts to prove behavioural RoI, we designated three classifications: Improved, Maintained and Excelled, reflecting the inconsistent motivations and competencies across the leadership hierarchy. These classifications allowed us to connect coaching impact to behaviours in the context of targets. They also enabled the organization to identify and assess individual leader behaviours as part of a strategy to improve retention and develop a culture of collective understanding. These classifications were allocated percentages which, when applied, provided a realistic estimation for net added value:

Figure 16: Behavioural classifications, definitions and percentages (replacing attributable-deadweight reckoning)

Behavioural status	Definition	Percentage
Improved	Short-term perspective Job over vocation Eschews organizational values	75%
Maintained	Balanced perspective Applies organizational values	50%
Excelled	Long-term vision High discretionary energy Lives by organizational values	25%

You will see from Figure 16, for those leaders where there is judged to be the greatest scope for development (Improved), the attached percentage represents an estimate of the coach's potential (attributable) impact, and so on (ceiling at 75% assumes that any leader deemed to be at 100% would not exist in the organization). It should also be noted that the language used for these classifications was carefully considered to avoid any implication of poor attitudes among the leadership cohort, in line with cultural sensitivities.

Getting to behavioural RoI

Emphasizing behavioural change in this way allowed us to switch the focus for evaluation of impact away from financial RoI to behavioural RoI. In other words, we were now able to go to the organization with evidence of behavioural change, resulting from coaching, to achieve tangible targets, to which monetary benefit could be allocated.

Table 30 represents the live calculation.

Table 30   Evaluation calculation

Investment	Impact points	Added value	Behavioural impact calculator (maintained)	Net added value
£750	Talent retention and promotion	£7,500	50%	£3,750
	Team restructuring	£22,000	50%	£11,000
	Improved performance (individual and team)	£36,000	50%	£18,000
	Cross-selling the organization	£25,000	50%	£12,500
				−£750
Total				£44,500

As with the previous case study, all impact points have been represented as tangible targets (organizational growth has been omitted) that are relatable to their intangible contributory factors in Table 28. These impact points are designed to be treated as wide categories that can be fine-tuned to fit the individual leader's outcome and development focus. Therefore, new initiatives, if relevant, would appear in the 'cross-selling' classification, as would recruitment. They are deliberately broad for flexibility, to be able to capture myriad individual leadership targets. Furthermore, the simplicity of this final calculation provides the stakeholder with an easy to access set of figures in terms of financial accountability.

In this case study, an estimated financial value of £44,500 was assigned to the original coaching investment for this manager. We have not represented this as a percentage increase on the basis that we consider any percentage of four figures unrelatable.

Stage 3: Retrieving strategic data (to inform organizational strategy and social RoI)

In the introduction to this chapter, we referred to the distinct attitude of sectors to evaluation and this case study goes some way to prove that the evaluator should never assume what is important to the client organization. Apart from reinforcing our assertion that the coach (evaluator) should immerse themselves in the internal context through fostering a collaborative relationship, this case is an example of how to arrive at an evaluation of the impact of leadership coaching on behaviours: behavioural return on investment. Due to the emphasis on what we were evaluating, the structure and format for the various frameworks were markedly different to those we used in the private sector case study. In the previous example, we commented on the final appearance of the evaluation framework as akin to an accountancy balance sheet. In this current case, the focus is much wider than the bottom line. What is clear is that any evaluation model needs to serve the organization by being relatable, both visually and in terms of a return on investment that is of interest.

The final meeting

At this final meeting with the team, we debriefed on the evaluation experience and the accountability data we had produced in line with assessing the impact on leadership behaviours. A system that was able to connect behaviours to tangible outcomes and provide meaningful monetization was roundly applauded. However, we were quick to point out that we had only honoured one part of our evaluation commitment and we now needed to turn our attention to the retrieval and dissemination of strategic data.

Early on in this process it was agreed that the holy grail for our evaluation system would be to reveal a societal return on investment, but that this would be some time in the making, as any such informant would require banks of data over a number of years. Therefore, we decide to temper our ambition and leave SRoI as a work in progress, while concentrating in the meantime on strategic data that would usefully inform the internal workings and future strategies of the organization. From this standpoint we produced Table 31 for discussion at our debrief meeting. The version below is a collective effort with the organization guiding the data retrieved from the evaluation to relevant destinations.

Final thoughts

This organization was especially complex, operating within two distinct environments – PIE and ambidextrous – a combination of which heightened the tensions around leadership, muddying the waters for coaching foci and exacerbating the challenge to evaluate impact. Therefore, in this case, despite the pressures of numerous external stakeholders to evaluate for financial accountability, the retrieval and strategic dissemination of data took centre stage, as a way of countering the general ambiguity over leadership outcomes and organizational expectations.

Table 31 Building a strategic database from evaluation

Impact points	Strategic data
Talent management	Retention strategies Evolving leadership behaviours Future development strategies
Team management (people leader)	Pivotal positions and priority leadership skills Promotions and career paths
Team management (team leader)	Capacity building Budgets and growth Developing SOM – silo busting
Long-term strategy	Long-term funding strategy Long-term donor strategy Future commercial partnerships Career development for ex-young people in poverty Employer partnerships Qualifications and accreditation Policy projects – research, influence and solutions Alumni groups Reliable evaluation system for impact of organization
For the coach	Advocacy for Level 5 leader Components of future programme design Evolving leadership outcomes

Guiding questions

Our focus on evaluation never ceases to unlock fascinating insights into the tensions, pressure points and challenges facing organizations. As a constant source of new knowledge, evaluation underlines its credentials as a vital informant for the wider strategy. However, for all the answers it provides, it raises an equal number of – often provocative – questions. Having worked with this organization we were gratified that we were able to put theory successfully into practice, but we left with a number of queries that were not directly related to the SRoI the organization craved, but were relevant to the wider debate around running a charity as a business. These questions revealed the stark reality of the challenge of ambidexterity in the third sector (and, indeed, in public sector organizations such as education), highlighting the relative convenience of evaluation for organizations focused on a singular primary goal for profit.

Although we do not claim to have solutions, two of these outstanding issues gave us food for thought and we learnt a lot from harnessing them to guide our evaluation design:

- Is it ever compatible with the skill sets and motivations of its leaders, to run a charity as a business?

Figure 17: Evaluation process flowchart

- First meeting with client to review existing leadership development programme and present Level 5 leadership model. **1 hour – all**
- Production of **Table 1** - environment for evaluation (evaluator's reference). **1 hour coach – evaluator**
- Application of evaluation levers to arrive at leadership outcomes, coaching foci and evaluation targets. **1 hour – coach evaluator**
- Second meeting to confirm **Table 2** and discuss strategic placement. **1 hour – all**
- Inventory of needs (**Table 3**). **30 minutes – coach evaluator**
- Coaching session with designated leader to agree individual outcomes and development needs (introducing connected evaluation criteria) **Table 4. 1 hour – coach and leadership candidate**
- Third meeting to unveil outcomes, coaching foci and evaluation framework to the (evaluation) team. **1 hour – all**
- Selecting relevant impact points and apportioning value. **Unspecified – sponsor**
- Evaluation assessment meeting with leader and organizational other (appraisal). **1 hour – leadership candidate, line manager**
- Final meeting – debrief and assessment of effectiveness of model to produce a behavioural RoI. **1 hour – all**
- Retrieval and dissemination of strategic data. **Ongoing – organization**

- Are the different motives of funders (government: statistical, corporate: brand) an impossible distraction for the organization trying to use evaluation to provide behavioural RoI and, ultimately, SRoI?

Evaluation flowchart

Estimated time spent on evaluation

- Leadership Development Collaboration (LDC) team – 4 hours (including review of existing programme, and presentation and implementation of Level 5 leadership model).
- Coach evaluator (including LDC meetings and charged one-to-one coaching sessions for objectives and assessment) – 6 hours.
- Leadership candidate – 2 hours (incorporated within coaching sessions and including appraisal).
- Sponsor/department head – unspecified.

9 Case study: Evaluating the impact of leadership coaching in a secondary school (evaluating the impact of coaching on potential and evaluation transferability)

Snapshot

Sector: Secondary school (state).
Governance: Board of governors and school senior leadership team.
Strategic focus: Improving status and reputation. Developing students as leaders of the future.
Culture: Values (school): respect, hard work and progress. Values (pupil): empowerment, connectedness, enterprise and transformation.
Brand: Member of the Activate Learning Education Trust (ALET) group of schools.
Evaluation focus: Evaluating the impact of leadership coaching on potential: How transferable is leadership coaching (and its evaluation) to young people?

Context and background

One of the key challenges for our evaluation system was whether or not it could be effectively transferable, and this was a significant driver for researching across different sectors. As a result of exploring diverse organizational landscapes, we inevitably collected a number of fascinating, unexpected insights into leadership, giving us access to new thinking and expectations for the future. One of the significant ideas to emerge from these insights was that, at a time when leadership talent is scarce and highly valued, young people are potentially the greatest untapped leadership resource we have. Our research inspired us to expand the scope of our leadership coaching purview to include youth leadership, working with schools and other youth organizations to provide coaching for young people at pivotal moments in their lives, specifically: the transition from primary to secondary education, and the transition from education to university or employment. Our studies revealed that many of the cognitive and emotional behaviours we were coaching in conventional leadership settings mirrored those needed by young people moving out of childhood into adulthood.

The GreenWing Project emerged from this thinking. Set up in 2018 to work with young people between the ages of 13–24, it provides leadership coaching focused on potential in an unstructured leadership environment, rather than experience in a formal leadership career setting. The results of early pilot programmes have been overwhelmingly positive and GreenWing predicts youth leadership will become a significant coaching opportunity for the future. Therefore, it makes sense that we should include one of these programmes in our portfolio of case studies, not only as a unique example of coaching evaluation, but as our most rigorous test so far, as to how well (or not) our theory is transferable.

GreenWing has been working with a state secondary school in the south of England since 2018, providing one-to-one and group leadership coaching for selected pupils as members of the senior student leadership cohort. In 2016 the school was labelled as 'underperforming' and 'failing', falling below the government's 'floor standard'. At this time, a new headteacher was recruited to turn the school around, focusing on standards and values to restore confidence (student and teacher) through development and support, engaging pupils, parents and teachers to create a positive learning environment. As part of the general improvement programme, it was also committed to the collection and dissemination of useful data to drive future strategy and performance.

We were initially introduced to the school as part of a 'recovery strategy'. It was quickly apparent that our ideas and approaches were strongly aligned with the vision of the headteacher, and it was agreed we should carry out a pilot programme (pro bono), supporting the school in achieving its goals. As a pioneering leadership coaching programme there was no template upon which we could draw, and both parties (the school and GreenWing) felt we would be starting from scratch: identifying leadership outcomes and behaviours for students to design a programme that was relevant, relatable and challenging (but achievable), including an evaluation system that simultaneously proved its worth and provided vital strategic data.

Our aim was to avoid various iterations of traditional school initiatives for the development of young people by focusing specifically on leadership, delivering coaching to a standard experienced by our established leadership clients. We also understood that we would be coaching leaders where very few leadership opportunities existed (beyond school posts). In other words, we were developing potential: a leadership mindset that anticipated long-term future roles rather than supporting current leaders in situ. An effective programme that held the attention of young people, with no promise of a leadership position at the end, was just one of the many new challenges that characterized our project and would exercise the collaborative mindset that we were about to forge with the school.

The collaborative experience: uncovering the context for evaluation

The coaching relationship was directly with the school's headteacher. A number of informal preliminary conversations had already taken place around the idea of a youth leadership coaching programme: where it might fit, criteria for candidates and what sort of outcomes we might expect. These were enthusiastic conversations as the concept of coaching fell easily into step with the school's overarching strategy to move from underperformance to high achievement. The collaborative relationship was seen as mutually beneficial: the prospect for the coach to pilot an exciting new project based on the idea that young people were an underused, underserved leadership resource, the characteristics of which could potentially redefine the future leadership landscape at a time of momentous change (post-Covid) – and a unique opportunity to align the rewritten values of the school with a practical programme of development that would impact on the students and the school's standing, both in educational terms, and as a positive contributor to the local community.

As a result of these informal discussions, a pilot programme was proposed. The leadership cohort was self-selecting, being the senior student leadership team for that year (head boy and head girl; deputy head girl and deputy head boy). The target at this early stage was to understand the impact of high-level leadership coaching on Year 13 students, and whether it actually worked – coaching leadership potential rather than leaders.

A word on youth leadership coaching (what we were trying to achieve)

The vision of the GreenWing Project is to empower young people to lead young people in a way that is relevant and relatable. However, it is worth going beyond the strapline to provide the reader with a snapshot of the overall concept, to explain the direction of the coaching, emerging outcomes and future foci for evaluation.

Youth leadership coaching focuses on the early development of a leadership mindset including: What is my leadership brand? What type of leader do I want to be? The actual programme is structured in three stages: Authentication (my leadership qualifications and brand); Development (my leadership tools) and Legacy (my leadership ambition). It is designed to get young people to think counter-intuitively about traditional leadership, and promotes a new set of outcomes and behaviours that are generally natural or instinctive to the candidate:

Figure 18: The characteristics of youth leadership

Traditional leadership	Youth leadership
Intuitive	Counter-intuitive
Experience	Potential
Tried and tested	Experimental
Short term	Long term
Confined	Unconfined
Timid (fear of failure)	Brave (a safe place to fail)
What?	Why?

Throughout this book, we have stated that leadership outcomes are a moving target, constantly evolving in a dynamic environment. The concept of youth leadership takes this assertion to another level of complexity, and we felt that it would be a missed opportunity not to present this pilot as an alternative (to more conventional interventions) case study. This study not only provides a current illustration of evolving leadership outcomes in a unique context, but, more generally, the transferability of leadership coaching across generations and, specifically, how well our evaluation theory adapts.

In this case study, the collaborative experience was a voyage of exploration and discovery, unlike the previous two case studies, seen as a contractual coming together between client and coach. As the programme developed, it was clear that evaluation of impact had a significant role to play, not solely to provide the financial and intellectual justification for an unknown quantity, but as a vital source of data, as one of the cornerstones upon which the school's overarching strategy was being built.

The evaluation environment

One of the recurring themes for this book is that evaluation strategies are limited because evaluators fail to move beyond a one-size-fits-all mentality. In this case study, we rigorously test our evaluation theory in terms of its adaptability and transference to a unique organizational leadership coaching context, as one of our key criteria for a successful evaluation system. To begin with, we were certain that a literal application of our theory would not work. In this example, the reader is invited to share our sense of experimentation, and experience in real time the dexterity needed when applying these ideas (to their own unique evaluation contexts).

We started by removing all preconceptions, stripping back ideas about leadership, coaching and evaluation, to produce a new set of definitions. To do this, we asked a series of questions:

- How might our understanding of the influence of the evaluation environment change?
- How adaptable could our evaluation levers become?
- What does ambidexterity mean in this context?
- What are the leadership outcomes (and coaching dimensions) we were seeking?

These questions recognized that all descriptors (problem areas, evaluation levers, etc.) would potentially take on a significantly different meaning (as opposed to the more nuanced distinctions in previous case studies), and we were interested in how easily (or not) these criteria were reinterpreted as part of our general assessment of transferability. Accordingly, we set out to follow the logical sequence of our evaluation theory, but reframed around these seminal questions.

What is the evaluation environment and does it matter?

From our preliminary conversations with Laure, the school's headteacher, evaluation was a footnote to the idea of introducing a high-level leadership coaching programme, and seen solely as a mechanism to unlock possible funding and justify budgetary destination. Throughout our work in the education sector, it is thematic that coaching and leadership are welcomed with open arms as part of a future vision for schools and young people, and yet budgetary allocation is either reluctantly granted, or set at a bare minimum. Alternatively, the quality of coaching is underestimated: makeshift – loosely interpreted by well-meaning but unqualified members of staff who have scant knowledge (usually reliant on a version of Whitmore's GROW Model) – or focused on traditional generic youth development programmes. Perhaps one of the reasons for a lack of intellectual and financial commitment might be, dare we posit, that the idea students are receiving a level of coaching far and beyond anything experienced by their teachers is a difficult concept to grasp or accommodate.

As with the case study in Chapter 8, evaluation was one part of a wider coaching programme proposal. Unlike other case studies, however, there was no semblance of a recognizable coaching or leadership culture, the only guidelines being the espoused values of the school (which, as with most organizations, were open to multiple interpretations or understandings). Within this context, the first question we asked ourselves was did the environment for evaluation actually matter, or could we bypass this part of the process? To answer this, we kept to our tried-and-tested sequential process, to see where it took us, starting with a definition of the unique organizational context.

To reveal the organizational context, we applied our evaluation levers in the usual way to our four benchmark problem areas: data usage, dissemination, timelines and competency. In organizations with an established coaching culture, a traditional leadership structure and a subsequent desire to evaluate the impact of coaching investments, these four problem categories are self-explanatory. However, in this particular context, we found that they appear not as problems, but as positives, inviting the collaborators to imagine new opportunities for student development via leadership coaching. This realization distinguishes youth leadership coaching as a unique development methodology that captures the educational zeitgeist (and beyond), and in this case acts as a cornerstone in the rebuilding of the school's reputation, growing its status and attracting and retaining pupils and teaching talent.

Accordingly, we reframed these four categories as questions: How useful would it be to have data on student leadership development and how best to use it? Who should take responsibility for gathering and disseminating data and how can we use this data to the advantage of the school and community? What would be the most useful timings to evaluate the impact of the coaching, and would this be a key component in attracting ex-pupils to an effective alumni group? What is measurable (in practical terms) that is also worth measuring?

On data usage

When asked, the school felt it needed to evaluate the impact of this programme and make best use of the data for three reasons. Firstly, for what it was: a pioneering idea in which they were at the forefront – leading the way. Secondly, as evidence for funding in a highly competitive market with limited resources at a time when there are many fads and popular buzzwords competing for attention, and funders are suspicious of creative ideas without a track record. Thirdly, for marketing and rebranding the school as part of a wider strategy to move from a 'failing' to 'high-achieving' status.

On dissemination

In our discussions with the school, numerous useful outlets for evaluation data were identified. From the school's perspective, evaluation data would facilitate a headline marketing opportunity that would spotlight the school's contribution to youth development in the broader educational spectrum. In their own words:

> If we can prove we are doing something no one else is, doing it well, so that it really has an impact on our students and their futures, then we need to use that data to tell our story and make us famous.

In addition, evaluation data would be used to recruit students and the best teaching talent, while good news stories were also felt to be inspiring to younger students considering continuing their education into sixth form and beyond. Apart from this, there were more obvious, official outlets to secure status and funding.

On timelines

As the GreenWing Project itself was at a developmental stage, the collaborative process allowed us to explore new ideas directly with the school. Together, we visualized the coaching across a wider timeline than initially imagined, from Year 7 to Year 13. Both these age ranges were considered to be pivotal times in a young person's life: from primary to secondary education; from childhood to adulthood. In essence, there was every possibility that, if successful, leadership coaching would span the entire (secondary) academic life of the student, covering different aspects of leadership development at different times. In the first instance it was envisaged that the programme would focus on Years 12 and 13, where an obvious leadership cohort was already in place, and here the coaching would be designed to provide support and development.

At the same time, a second less obvious, but equally impactful, target group was identified to have a claim on coaching. This group was not so clearly differentiated and, along with the standout go-to leaders, there were also the shy ones, those finding their way, the disruptors, the underperformers, etc. If we were to be true to our principles and really believe that leadership was about potential, we were underestimating the size of the talent pool to be trawled in early years coaching. Accordingly, expanding the purview of leadership coaching meant that we had created an additional timeline challenge to which evaluation data would very usefully inform strategies, especially post-school and alumni groups.

On competency

As we were starting with a clean slate, there was an opportunity, as well as a clear directive, to concentrate on measuring impact on things that count. Therefore, the school was looking for an uncomplicated system that was practical and informative of clearly defined areas of interest. In this case, competency to evaluate was not seen as a challenge but as an opportunity to extend the teaching staff, giving them responsibility to supervise and become engaged with the coaching. It was assumed that most data would be collected from the individual leader and that, in itself, was seen as an entry point for teachers to get involved in more in-depth, one-to-one engagements with the pupils – satisfying their original vocational motives for joining the profession.

Reimagining evaluation levers

We wanted to adhere to the basic principles of our evaluation process as much as possible, and this meant, if we were to apply evaluation levers to our four problem areas, now reoriented as opportunities, we would similarly need to reimagine and redefine them. We wondered how these would emerge and whether they would even be relevant to evaluation in this context. This was a key moment in our experiment to test how readily transferable our theory was. These levers were discussed as part of the collaborative process, using the original headings and the intuitive interpretations of the headteacher, before placing our own spin on them, to fit this particular context for evaluation, as illustrated by the findings and resultant table below.

- **Primary goal**

For the school, the basis for a primary goal was to consider the individual outcomes of students along with those of the school, and align the two. The school's vision and primary goal was to transform lives through education. Broken down, this meant it was committed to supporting its young people in achieving aspirational next-step destinations, through both qualifications and a sound belief in self-worth. In turn, this would enhance the school's success and growing reputation as part of the ALET (Activate Learning Education Trust) group of schools and its place in the top echelons of sixth form schools.

- **Evaluation status**

The focus for evaluation status was not on formal or informal (obviously none existed), but on the teachers and how they would react to being a part of the project. The school saw evaluation status as a professional growth opportunity and an entry point for a closer mentoring relationship with students. This was seen as a positive, reflecting various feedback from teacher appraisals about limited openings for increased responsibility and pupil engagement. Therefore, the delegation of evaluation responsibilities was seen as an opportunity.

- **Multigenerational leadership pools**

This was largely covered in the previous section on *timelines*. In this context, the idea of multigenerational leadership pools is far more conceptual and is used to characterize the whole notion of leadership coaching for young people where, if you scratch the surface, you realize different opportunities and different definitions of leadership potential, at all ages.

- **Organizational context**

Organizational context was found to be an operating tension that fell into two defining categories:

a As a school, the organization is governed by conventional educational boundaries.
b The espoused values that students are encouraged to abide by (from personal choice).

The headteacher encapsulates this tension perfectly:

You could say we are driven by a strong culture, defined by our values, set within a rigid operational structure.

From these initial responses, we were able to re-visualize our evaluation levers in the context of the school:

Figure 19: Reimagined evaluation levers

Original evaluation lever	Reimagined evaluation lever
Primary goal	Student academic and personal achievement School results and reputation
Evaluation status	Professional development opportunity for teachers increasing scope of meaningful responsibility
Multigenerational leadership pools	Authentication and development strategies at pivotal times in students' school careers
Organizational context	Emphasis on culture through school values in the context of rigid educational structure

From the application of reimagined levers to the four problem areas (now reframed as opportunities), Table 32 emerged as a representation of the evaluation environment. Unlike previous case studies, this table was presented at a meeting with the headteacher, specifically to open discussions on outcomes and the ambidextrous challenges facing students participating in the programme.

We concluded that exploring the evaluation environment was useful and remained an essential part of the process. In an organization where no leadership structure exists, and unstated primary goals are shared between three stakeholders (the school, the student, the government), this was the first opportunity for the school to sit down and formally begin to pull together different priorities, placing them in an ambidextrous context.

As we developed this table, we were aware that the opportunity and the coaching focus columns were a little disconnected, because of the overlap between the students and the sponsors, specifically where the emergent opportunities focused on the outcomes for the school rather than the young person. However, the introduction of an ambidextrous perspective made sense of these focal points, in terms of young people's leadership outcomes and the focus for the coach, while the opportunity column began to formulate the criteria for evaluation. Unsurprisingly, this table formed the agenda for a fascinating and lively meeting between the coach and the sponsor as a prequel to the design of the programme.

Table 32 The context for evaluation

Opportunity area	Evaluation lever	Emergent dimension of opportunity	Ambidextrous leadership and coaching focus
Data usage	Primary goal	As education pioneers To be financially competitive To enhance the reputation and status of the school	Personal achievement balanced with contribution to the school
Dissemination	Evaluation status	To develop and retain teaching talent To broaden the responsibility and increase the effectiveness of teachers through one-to-one mentoring opportunities	Managing up balanced with managing down
Timelines	Multigenerational leadership pools	Continued offering of support after school and formation of strong alumni group	Authentication or development stages of coaching
Competency	Organizational context	Evaluating the things we value	Cultural outcomes (values) versus wider academic and educational targets

The design experience

Stage 1: Designing an evaluation framework: connecting leadership and coaching outcomes to evaluation targets

We have seen how effectively our evaluation tools have flexed across the unique organizational context, and this has vindicated the time spent examining in detail the evaluation environment. Emerging from this preliminary groundwork, Table 33 begins to connect coaching outcomes to evaluation, having reoriented problematics (which now appear as unique evaluation opportunities in the first column) and reimagined levers.

This table (Table 33) provides a really clear sight of both youth leadership coaching outcomes (remembering there is no existing template for these, therefore the importance is emphasized) and evaluation targets that are relevant and helpful to the school. Unlike other case studies, the emphasis of this table is on the design, content and approach of the coaching programme, and evaluation as an opportunity (as opposed to a problem to be solved). This table formed the basis of our third formal collaborative meeting.

Table 33 Connecting coaching outcomes to evaluation targets by applying evaluation levers to unique evaluation opportunities

Unique evaluation opportunities	Dimensions and insights for leadership coaching	Influential lever	Ambidextrous dimension for evaluation target
Evaluation environment	Identifying and supporting a leadership mindset Contributing to a wider leadership role Ambidextrous leadership behaviours/judgement	Primary goal Organizational context	Academic achievements Personal achievements Alignment with school values
Bias and contradiction	N/A	N/A	N/A
Responsibility	Managing-up to facilitate teacher mentoring	Evaluation status	Mentoring relationship: Teachers
Quality of data	Individual areas of leadership responsibility Impact points	Primary goal Evaluation status	Performance against designated areas of leadership responsibility Performance against impact points Educational data
Generational reach	Developing coaching behaviours in leadership role Authenticating individual leadership credentials Developing unique leadership behaviours	Multigenerational leadership pools	Mentoring younger students Continuing to sixth form Continuing to university Community leadership roles Academic results (GCSEs/A levels)
Timelines	Identifying leadership ambitions (short, medium, long term)	Multigenerational leadership pools Organizational context	Alumni groups Requests for coaching support beyond school Returnee (ex-pupil) coaching and contribution to school and community

What about bias and contradiction?

We spent some time pondering our six benchmark categories (opportunities) as part of the transition to the unique coaching context. The only classification we felt was probably not appropriate was *bias and contradiction*. For the sake of symmetry, we have included it in Table 33, and another evaluator taking on a similar task may well find that it is relevant and applicable under certain circumstances. However, we felt that shooing it in overcomplicated an already complex concept; after all, we had been commissioned to produce a framework that was user-friendly.

In our deliberations we considered the bias and contradiction pressure points for the school and these were mainly found in the tension between distinct outcomes for the school and outcomes for the young leader. We saw in Table 32 how a lens of ambidexterity crystallized and aligned the two sets of interest and we would argue that this sufficiently negated *bias and contradiction* for our purposes at this time. It could be claimed that the external stakeholders (local authority, government, etc.) provide a source of bias by dictating outcomes that serve their own purposes, potentially at odds with the vision of the school. However, we felt that the focus of the impact of our coaching was on the young leader and any outcome conflict that might create either bias or contradiction was between the school and the external stakeholder.

Where the evaluation model might fit: setting the tone

The main distinction in this case study is that the concept of leadership does not preoccupy those benefiting from leadership coaching. Due to the absence of a relatable primary goal to drive leadership development, leadership is arguably a nebulous idea, to which evaluation provides some structure, overarching a new set of outcomes, targets, goals and expectations, hitherto unfamiliar, for both the young leader and the school establishment. In this capacity, evaluation opens the door to a gentler, more informal collaborative experience for the coach, coachee and sponsor, recognizing the individual's exploration of leadership instincts and natural behaviours, rather than the conventional template for leadership that often characterizes established hierarchical mindsets.

With no existing leadership structure or strategy chain to work with, how would this affect where we placed our evaluation framework? Fitting the evaluation component into the organizational strategy has always been a key part of our theory, specifically to facilitate its role as a valuable source of strategic data. However, as we thought about this, we considered the sensitivities attached to coaching young people and felt evaluation potentially had a different role to perform once strategically integrated, namely, in setting the tone for the coaching programme.

Here, we deliberately departed from our original concept of evaluation as a vital cog in the strategic machine, simultaneously aligning strategy and acting as a strategic informant, appropriately inserted into the system. Instead, we saw evaluation in terms of a conductor of an orchestra, focused on intangibles such as tone, tempo and volume, as part of a less formal, collaborative approach to goal setting. Therefore, in this case, we envisaged our evaluation system as implicit, overarching the coaching process in three stages:

- Stage 1 – Introduced at the outset of the coaching engagement (Table 32)
- Stage 2 – Capturing evaluation data (see later Tables 35 and 36)
- Stage 3 – Application of value to impact points (see later Table 38)

An inventory of needs: necessary or useful?

As we continued to follow our sequence of evaluation theory, our next potential shortcut was whether we could do away with an inventory of needs. In previous case studies (and more generally), an inventory of needs facilitates the practical design for a system to be workable for the unique internal context of

Table 34 Using evaluation levers to reveal an inventory of needs to exploit opportunities

Evaluation lever	Definition	Opportunity (emerging from internal context)	Inventory of needs (to exploit opportunities)
Primary goal	School reputational growth through student achievement	Pioneering approach to student development	Justification: evidence of impact for funding, pupil incentivization and school status
Evaluation status	Designated teacher	Development opportunity for teachers to provide meaningful engagements (higher job satisfaction)	Data for teacher reward and recognition systems
Multigenerational	Distinct authentication or development programmes	Early empowerment strategies Leadership development acceleration	Flexibility to switch between programmes
Organizational context	Emphasis on values in a rigid educational environment	Accommodating student and teacher ambitions and vocation through focus on intangible values as a means to achieving tangible targets	Consistent ambidextrous judgements to legitimize values-driven behaviours to achieve external educational targets

the organization. The inventory of needs is a direct response to the organizational blind spots emerging from the internal context. However, the developing theme of this case is that blind spots, problematics, barriers, etc. are all reframed positively as opportunities. Therefore, we adjusted our framework, replacing 'blind spots' with 'opportunities' and reorienting the 'inventory of needs' column to represent potential entry points to exploit opportunities:

We were surprised and encouraged to see our inventory shift from its original modus operandi to a strategic function. Here, the final column provides a level of strategic insight so far missing in the organization, crystallizing goals and strategies, refocusing on outcomes for evaluation rather than operational evaluation functionality. Having performed this exercise, we found that this stage of our process was both necessary and useful, and we would recommend that any evaluator take the time to formulate such an inventory. What we learnt from this case was that the inventory framework is organic, and that allows it the agility to develop naturally along a practical/strategic continuum, dependent on the evaluation environment.

The evaluation experience

Stage 2: Data collection

In this case study we were aiming to evaluate the impact of leadership coaching on young people in a school setting, where there is no conventional primary goal, multiple stakeholder interest and leadership as an unfamiliar concept. We focused on a member of the senior leadership team (Year 13, head girl), Catherine, who was informed at the end of Year 12 that she would be appointed to a leadership role. As part of her promotion, she was invited to a preliminary meeting (with the headteacher and the head of sixth form) to discuss her personal outcomes and ambitions for the role, how the school's values might influence her leadership, and her designated area of specific responsibility: student culture, leadership and community. Also, at this meeting, the idea of a leadership coach to support and develop Catherine's leadership was introduced, and she was engaged in a further discussion about her perceived potential challenges and possible areas of personal development.

Table 35 is the resultant ambidextrous framework. We have adapted this accordingly, and replaced the subordinate strategy column with Catherine's designated area of responsibilities (including scholastic achievement). The coaching focus column was less formal (than previous case studies) in this first instance, reflecting the absence of the coach at the meeting. We formulated this framework from the feedback we received from the preliminary meeting with Catherine and presented it for discussion at our next collaborative session where, together, we confirmed that outcomes were aligned, agreed the coaching focus, and completed the evaluation criteria column (the strategic data, as with other case studies, remained incomplete). Finally, the coach met with

Catherine for an introductory session at which Table 35 formed the agenda (in our experience with young leaders, this was a useful framework to break the ice, providing structure and direction in an unfamiliar setting).

Table 35   Evaluation framework for Catherine (head girl)

Designated responsibility	Exploitative leadership targets	Explorative leadership targets	Leadership coaching focus	Evaluation criteria	Strategic data
Culture	Anti-bullying	Mentoring	Coaching behaviours for leadership	Reported bullying data Mentoring initiatives	
Leadership	Operational (immediate)	Strategic (legacy)	Develop personal leadership brand: Organizational Strategic thinking Communication	(Re-) structure of student senior leadership team events Initiatives (school)	
Community	School and local	Creative and innovative initiatives	Public speaking Macro-Knowl. development	Events Initiatives (community)	
Scholar (ambidextrous)	Academic achievements	Personal achievements	Ambidextrous behaviours: judgement prioritization Time management	A level results University placement	

Table 35 continues to develop the idea of building ambidextrous chains but, in this case, where there is a less formal leadership assessment process, the links serve to inform evaluation criteria (rather than legitimize counter-intuitive outcomes or targets). Throughout this case study, evaluation has been characterized by a tension between what is valuable for the school and what is valuable for the student. The ambidextrous chains make sense of this tension by aligning the two sets of values. When we reviewed the table we had produced, we noticed that, at face value, the evaluation column was weighted towards school goals, except for the final category (scholar) which defined ambidexterity from a young leader's perspective. However, we were satisfied our model connected both sets of outcomes to common goals, and this was the moment when we realized that our concept of youth leadership was structurally viable, the impact of which we would be able to evaluate.

The leadership coaching experience

In Table 36 we have arrived at a workable leadership outcome framework template, not dissimilar to the type we would expect to find in any private, public or third sector leadership system. The outcomes and contribution (to a primary goal) have been agreed with Catherine (at her meeting with the headteacher and the head of sixth form) and developed from Table 35 as a relatable, real-life synthesis of targets emanating from her designated responsibilities. In this pilot, the coach will faithfully record the content of Catherine's coaching sessions and is responsible for completing the second column. Finally, Catherine is asked to complete the third column at the end of the programme.

Table 36 Evaluation data-collection template

Agreed outcomes	Coaching dimensions	Demonstrable impact	Contribution to a primary goal
Develop personal leadership brand			To promote a leadership culture throughout the school
To lead the student leadership team			To reposition authority throughout the school, encouraging senior school members to take responsibility, as part of the transition to HE or the workplace
To represent pupils and liaise with senior staff			To listen to the 'voice of the school' and give wider ownership for school policies
To improve inclusivity at all levels across the school			To promote well-being through engagement To celebrate diversity
To be an ambassador			To attract new students To uphold the values of the school
Personal ambidexterity			Academic achievement School reputation and status

Table 37 is the returned form, completed:

Table 37 Completed evaluation data-collection form

Agreed outcomes	Coaching dimensions	Demonstrable impact	Contribution to a primary goal
Develop personal leadership brand	Self-awareness Perspective: awareness of others EQ (emotional intelligence) for empathy and rapport Confidence through knowledge Valuing self	Through coaching I have developed an understanding of my leadership strengths and the values I hold. This has given me the confidence to be my own kind of leader and that has helped me make decisions which I am proud to stand by. This confidence has also allowed me to communicate effectively with my colleagues and this has helped me in all my leadership tasks so far. See below.	To promote a leadership culture throughout the school
To lead the student senior leadership team	Organizational skills Delegation Strategic thinking	I have worked closely with others in the senior leadership team. We meet once a week as a group and once every two weeks with reps from Years 12,11,10 and 9. This is a new format that I've set up. The wider group meeting is designed to be solution-based, and we are not looking to present the school with problems, only answers or suggestions. Other members of the senior leadership team take turns in running the meeting so that it's not just me.	To reposition authority throughout the school, encouraging senior school members to take responsibility, as part of the transition to HE or the workplace
To represent pupils and liaise with senior staff	Communication Managing-up How to be an influencer	As a result of the wider meetings we hold, I liaise with the Dep. Head once every two weeks. This was difficult at first because of her time commitments but now we put a regular date in the diary to meet and this has helped. I think it's important to present a positive outlook to the senior staff I talk to, even when we are discussing difficult issues.	To listen to the 'voice of the school' and give wider ownership for school policies

To improve inclusivity at all levels across the school	Organization Strategic initiatives through creativity and innovation Long-term strategic thinking Advanced delegation Communication	I have improved engagement with the non-school uniform days by asking students to suggest charities that they might like us to support. We will rotate these charities each time we hold a non-school uniform day. The first of these was a great success compared to the responses we were getting last year. I have asked other school leaders to take responsibility for this year's school events, including the prom. We are looking to form committees for each event, including students at all levels, and asking for suggestions. I have spoken to the whole school in my role as head girl at the first assembly and I intend to do this at least twice a term. My main message is that I want lower years to feel included in the student decision-making in the school: something we never had.	To promote well-being through engagement To celebrate diversity
To be an ambassador	Public speaking and presentation	I have attended the school open day where we met with new and prospective parents. I also gave a speech at this event outlining our exciting plans for the future.	To attract new students To uphold the values of the school
Personal ambidexterity	Time management Prioritization Judgement	I have enjoyed my leadership role and have managed to balance my extracurricular duties with my studies, maintaining high grades	Academic achievement School reputation and status

Impact points and an evaluation framework

For the final stage in our evaluation process we set out to identify impact points as destinations for Catherine's leadership, against which the impact of coaching would be evaluated. These impact points were targets for Catherine's leadership performance, emerging from her designated areas of responsibility, while, in this final iteration, demonstrable impact was a collation of self- and sponsor-assessment:

Table 38 Shared evaluation form

Impact point	Coaching dimension	Demonstrable impact	Contribution to an organizational target or a primary goal	Value dimension
Academic	**Leadership ambidexterity: balancing outcomes; prioritization; judgement** Preparing to make a wider contribution with your leadership **Making (career) choices aligned to your leadership**	**Results and university placement** Workplace experience **Teacher feedback**	A level results and university placements (league tables)	Ofsted report and rating
Student culture	Delegation **Organizational** Communication **Collaboration and inclusivity** Empowering versus Enabling	Successfully organized school events **Promoted anti-bullying initiative**	Anti-bullying strategy	Status Reputation Student recruitment
School community	**Strategic thinking** Culture (of collective understanding) **Presentation skills** Creativity and innovation **Management** Delegation	School ambassador **Led school groups and instigated working committees** Set up school pupil mentoring programme for younger years **Formalized pupil/ teacher communication**	Raise school profile in local community **Student engagement policy**	Sponsorship and commercial networks Community influence Reputation
Wider community	**Wider strategic thinking** The influence of knowledge as a leadership tool **Leadership legacy**	Attended external youth organization meetings **Member of local forum for youth in town** Contributed articles to local and national media	**Enhance wider reputation of school** Student recruitment	National recognition

In this case study, each impact point was under the sponsorship of a teacher or head of department (as part of the opportunity to extend teacher responsibilities to include meaningful one-to-one interactions – see Tables 32 and 33, dissemination and responsibility). The value dimensions were agreed and set by the senior leadership team (staff).

Stage 3: Disseminating data

Monetizing impact: does it matter?

In short, yes it does – but, unlike previous case studies, we are not attempting to monetize the value dimensions of impact in this instance. By not doing so, we are not saying that these cannot be financially assessed. However, as part of a first-year pilot, trying to conveniently shoo-in figures into the values column, felt like a specious exercise, and our educated guesswork was not a sufficient premise upon which to present the reader with a set of reliable calculations. Suffice to say, at this nascent stage (for youth leadership coaching), the evaluation agenda is one-dimensional, focused on accountability or funding. Furthermore, we accept that the value dimension for schools is more difficult to monetize, as many of the outcomes are reputational or politically motivated (owned by an external stakeholder); however, we believe that the exercise of placing a financial gain on the impact of coaching will continue to add structure and focus in an unfamiliar setting, where, arguably, it is most needed. Adding a monetary dimension to evaluation in this context is certainly something we would expect to see as the norm, in the future.

In time, we envisage, as part of the collaborative design of the programme and the integrated status of evaluation, the sponsor/teacher will be invited to provide financial assessments for hard outcomes to do with accountability or funding, and once these have been understood and set they will be readily applicable (subject to some fine-tuning) in future years. With regard to intangible outcomes (reputation, status, community, etc.), these are considered longer-term assessments, say over five years, and will be accessible through a growing bank of strategic data. Similarly, long-term evaluation focused on the achievements of alumni will belong to this databank, supplemented by a developing and thriving post-school community.

As part of any future evaluation calculations, we would still recommend the application of some form of attributable-deadweight reckoner for accuracy. In the case of a school, this may reflect the current status or position in league tables or other existing data (university placements, exam results, continuing to sixth form, student/staff recruitment/retention, etc.). There is also an opportunity to use student assessments, especially where the coaching is focused on the early stage leadership 'authentication' section of the programme, where candidates are taken from a wider pool of potentials, including some counter-intuitive categories such as disruptors or underachievers. In this context, the impact of the coach might arguably be at its highest point.

Destination of strategic data

Table 39 illustrates the destination of strategic data. The reader will see that, despite this being a pilot of a pioneering programme, a rich vein of strategic data is already available. In this simple framework, data is directly connected to impact points which ensures the whole process continues to be strategically aligned. Finally, the eventual destination of data is naturally in the gift of the school.

Table 39   Destination of strategic data

Impact points	Strategic data
Academic	**Coachee:** Does leadership empower students to achieve grades (or distract)? Career development Higher education support Long-term career tracking **School:** Teacher development Government and sponsor targets
Student culture	Living and working by the values of the school Young people leading young people A positive learning environment
School community	Anti-bullying policy School engagement (pupil/parent/teacher) Alumni network
Wider community	Commercial strategies Community strategies
For the coach	Advocacy for youth leadership concept Design and structure of future programmes Coaching methodologies New leadership outcomes

Final thoughts

In the widest sense, this programme proved to us that youth leadership coaching is highly impactful and that the impact can be evaluated. More specifically, we had evidence that our evaluation theory was easily transferable across even the most unconventional leadership coaching programmes.

Our experience of this particular internal context was that it was character-ized by the fact that teachers are generally time poor (or poor time managers) and lack an entrepreneurial sense of initiative for projects outside the school curriculum. Therefore, we were left to ponder how arduous and user-friendly the process (of evaluation) was, to be practical.

To the first point, we found that the programme was driven by the enthusi-asm and the energy of the headteacher as the main point of collaboration. We found that other department heads' level of involvement depended on receiv-ing an explicit directive from Laure (the headteacher). Therefore, the collabo-rative relationship was akin to a partnership, co-opting various relevant members of staff when required. In theory there was not a great call on staff resources to complete this programme; however, without the drive of Laure, the programme would probably still be running and incomplete. This did prove to us that teachers have their own high-level ambidextrous tension (similar to the third sector), where the reason they joined the profession gets skewed by the short-term targets of external stakeholders. Accordingly, before any such programme is undertaken, we would strongly advise that the coach evaluator finds a 'champion' with some significant authority in the school, to work with and promote the project.

Secondly, we were determined to design a programme that was simple and user-friendly. By 'user-friendly', we mean able to absorb the potential sensitivi-ties of coaching young people. In the first case study, we commented on the natural inclination for the organization to view evaluation as an accountancy spreadsheet, therefore our approach was to create a framework that was both familiar and spoke to the client in a language they readily understood. In this case, where the young leader is under the wing of the client (as opposed to being integrated in the existing leadership structure or hierarchy), we focused on the young person and wanted to produce a system that would allow them to comfortably be involved and take some ownership of their development. In turn, we found this approach set the tone of the programme and allowed us to design an evaluation model that was accessible to both the young leader and the associated teaching staff.

At the end of the programme, we were left with two unknowns. Firstly, was the focus on the development of the student, at a time when teacher develop-ment is limited to 'off-the-shelf' training (as opposed to individual coaching), a potential problem or a future challenge? Secondly, to be taken seriously, due to the general mindset of those working in education, does any future youth leadership coaching programme need to formally appear in budgets and be accepted as part of the school curriculum? Evaluation will no doubt provide us with the data to be able to answer these two questions, but not for some time.

Evaluation flowchart

Figure 20: Evaluation process flowchart

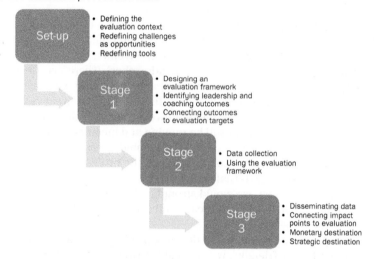

Set-up
- Defining the evaluation context
- Redefining challenges as opportunities
- Redefining tools

Stage 1
- Designing an evaluation framework
- Identifying leadership and coaching outcomes
- Connecting outcomes to evaluation targets

Stage 2
- Data collection
- Using the evaluation framework

Stage 3
- Disseminating data
- Connecting impact points to evaluation
- Monetary destination
- Strategic destination

Estimated time spent on evaluation

- Collaborative meetings between coach and headteacher – ongoing (for future programmes, allocate 1–2 hours).
- Coach evaluator (excluding ongoing collaborative meetings) – 2 hours (design), 2 hours (chargeable one-to-one coaching sessions: objectives and assessment).
- Leadership candidate – 2 hours (incorporated within preliminary and final coaching sessions and including student appraisal); ongoing feedback communication with teacher mentor.
- Other members of staff – unspecified (minimal).

10 Case study: Evaluating the impact of leadership coaching to embed productivity and well-being in commercially focused public services

Snapshot

Sector: Public service (with commercial focus).
Governance: Directors of customer services (ultimately metropolitan borough council board of directors).
Strategic focus: Improving service outcomes and well-being.
Culture: Accountability (and targets/outcomes) and responsibility (resilience and well-being).
Brand: Award-winning for customer service and service improvement.
Evaluation focus: Evaluating the impact of leadership coaching which values improvement as well as employee well-being.

Context and background

In this final case study we wanted to describe how the framework might work with a bigger principle in mind: that in any form of evaluation, the act of measurement can impact what is being measured. One of the most well known studies that raised our awareness of this involved the Hawthorne experiments. Famously, the study in Hawthorne (Chicago) in the 1970s was designed to examine the effects of shop-floor lighting on worker productivity in a manufacturing plant (Adair 1984). The experiments found a dubious link between lighting levels and productivity: productivity increased when the lighting levels were raised, but also when the lighting was dimmed. The study not only demonstrated a false link between lighting and productivity, but how the *act of measurement* can change behaviour, because it is being evaluated.

Known as the Hawthorne effect, such a feature of human behaviour may make it very difficult to create a reliable link between a cause and effect, but this does not discount that the act of measurement changes behaviour and that this can be used towards desired or desirable outcomes during and after the evaluation process. The Hawthorne effect can often be seen in participatory or collaborative forms of evaluation, which can oftentimes appear more like an organizational development or change programme than a linear process of articulating outcomes. This case study also presents a different way of thinking about the concept of collaboration, introducing a participatory approach as an alternative perspective for the evaluator to consider. Participatory forms of evaluation can be particularly useful where a wider change needs to happen across an organization or unit within it, and where there is the possibility of divergent views. Creative or imaginative methods – such as drawing or use of objects as metaphors – have also been used in these settings to articulate previously unarticulated or unknown outcomes, and where there is a need to emotionally support people through the process. Emotional support is an additional dimension for the evaluator to consider and make judgements upon, particularly when the topic of evaluation itself is sensitive or emotionally draining, or when there is a high possibility of conflict.

This case study is different to the others as it draws from a series of similar evaluation projects, to protect the identity of the organizations, teams and individuals involved in the process. Although it comprises multiple sources, it is presented as a single ethnographic study for pragmatic convenience (herein called 'Middleshire'). As such, Middleshire collates and pulls out common strands from practice to highlight key points from different leadership coaching evaluations, but retains a level of distance from specific events in specific organizations.

There were a number of commonalities in the projects selected to inform the case study presented here. Perhaps the most significant one was us being approached by a public service body to take a holistic view of the impact of leadership coaching, as part of a wider series of events, delivered by another team over a prolonged period (see also Chapter 8). At the time, the drive for productivity alongside well-being reflected a wider trend in the delivery of public services in the UK. As such, in each there was not just an interest in well-being as an outcome, but in well-being as part of the process of evaluation. In other words, the significant subtext for the evaluation process was to uncover the more positive aspects (intangibles) of impact beyond financial accountability. The aim in this case is to highlight how we used our ambidextrous framework for leadership coaching evaluation, to drive and embed the very strategic outcomes it seeks to measure.

As a footnote to this case study, we would also ask the reader to notice the different tone of the evaluation approach from an evaluator practitioner specifically tasked to produce an evaluation system that is not integrated into the current coaching and training programmes. This professional detachment (from the existing coaching) presents a different perspective that distinguishes this case study and provides evidence of the transferability of the evaluation theory to professionals not actively practising as coaches.

The collaborative experience: redefining collaboration as participation

Middleshire did not have the most positive of recent histories, both in terms of its delivery of key performance indicators and the work environment it had created for its staff. That said, new leadership was transforming productivity indicators, such as how long a local resident would wait for a response, or how soon an emergency would be addressed once a resident had logged an issue. The working culture had also significantly changed, through a concerted effort to build more positive teams and new ways of working. It was here that coaching, alongside a range of other training interventions, was commissioned for the leadership team at Middleshire Council's Customer Services Directorate. This leadership team as a collaboration (including heads of services within the directorate and team managers) was distinct from other case studies by being representative of a wider, more formal operational group (as opposed to a select strategic relationship at CEO status). This group was invited to choose which aspects of the training to engage in, such as self-management or how to manage own resilience and well-being. There was mixed engagement from Middleshire Council's leadership team during the coaching and training journey, as to be expected (varying attitudes to coaching), and some challenging experiences for all involved.

Our aim at Middleshire was to help them make sense of the impacts which had been delivered by an externally commissioned coaching team, and do so in a way which was sensitive to the wider drive towards employee, leader and manager well-being. In meetings with Middleshire, two potentially conflicting demands needed to be navigated. On the one hand, they wanted the credibility of someone external to the organization to help make an informed commentary about the impacts that had been generated through the coaching and training interventions; at the same time, they wanted them to work within the internal context and avoid a process that measured impact in a clinical, dissociated way which did not respect and value the voices of each individual in the directorate. In other words, they wanted to maintain the collaborative spirit that they had worked hard to develop over the last year through the leadership programme.

The evaluation environment

In this case study, we continue to push and test the applicability of our evaluation framework in a context where leadership coaching is part of a wider set of activity (e.g. alongside practical training delivered by an external company), and with the extra dimension that the evaluation process itself can help create the (positive) impacts it initially seeks to measure. Accordingly, we applied our evaluation levers to the four problem areas: data usage, dissemination, time-lines, and competency.

On data usage

In line with the culture of needing to be accountable and responsible for the use of public monies in the delivery and enhancement of public services, there was also a belief that investment in coaching and training needed to be justified. Therefore, the need for evaluation data was institutionally sanctioned. How-ever, the form and method of generating that data was not predetermined or heavily structured by the organization.

Middleshire, as a local government organization which is driven by account-ability and transparency, is data heavy. There were two types of data: firstly service related – for example, how long it takes to answer a call from a resident (a customer), time taken to resolve an issue, or number of outstanding calls awaiting response. Attached to these were clear targets and expectations related to this data, characterizing its institutional value. Secondly, there were data that were considered important, related to leader, manager, and employee well-being, such as sickness absences or grievances.

On dissemination

The executive of Middleshire's Customer Services Directorate had a clear pur-pose for the use of the evaluation. There was a general view that the leadership team was both visible and vocal about the achievements of their directorate, and had indeed secured awards for their transformation in quality of public services. Here, by commissioning an external organization to examine the impacts, there was a perception that this greater level of impartiality (com-pared to internal reports) would offer stronger credibility to the claims about achievement with the wider corporate leadership team at Middleshire, and therefore further build internal reputation and have a positive impact on the whole of the directorate in terms of brand and morale.

It was also recognized that this validated reputation could also have uses further afield, outside the organization, and across the sector, for future awards. However, at the same time this also highlighted a strong need (or belief) from the leadership team that the process of the evaluation should have beneficial effects on the team; otherwise there was a risk that the evaluation itself could dampen the positive changes in working practices and well-being that had already been generated through the coaching and training intervention. It per-haps also reflected a strong trust (and expectation) in the evaluation team to skilfully turn any criticisms and negative impacts of the programme into posi-tive outcomes.

On timelines

The coaching and training intervention had lasted a year and, during this period, impacts had been typically assessed through levels of satisfaction (e.g.

happy sheets). In the context of attempting to help people manage well-being in a highly pressurized quasi-commercial environment with targets, this seemed an appropriate way of measuring immediate impacts. In addition, impacts were also informally shared with the leadership team during the process (as is often the case with impacts generated through leadership coaching). Typical examples included individual leaders changing their working patterns during the day to be able to manage their own levels of stress, which they noticed had positively impacted their productivity as well as their relationships with others.

There was a particular focus on the day-to-day timeline of events and impacts, thereby highlighting the importance of habits and habit formation in the longer-term aspects of health and well-being. However, in commissioning the evaluation, it was clear that the leadership team was seeking a more collective, longer-term view. In addition, it also became apparent that evaluation had a role in attempting to deepen the learning and changes, and cascade that learning to others. However, the precise detail of timelines in this were not yet clear.

On competency

The leadership team felt they had some ability to evaluate claims of impact through the informal conversations they were having in their day-to-day working. They recognized this was not the most academic approach (scientifically rigorous) but it was sufficient to make a professional judgement about the quality of the coaching and training being delivered, and the potential further investment in their leadership team at different levels. The evaluation was not driven by a major concern around their own competency to deliver, but rather the perceived competency of them (as an internal body with a vested interest in telling a good story) as evaluation practitioners compared to a specialist evaluator with expert knowledge and reputation in the field (who might also be seen as more independent and impartial).

Through discussions, it is also important to note that the leadership team displayed a curiosity about what a participatory and imaginative approach to evaluation might look like in practice – how it might embed more deeply the positive change and enable them to build momentum and energy as these changes and behaviours were cascaded down.

Evaluation levers

In continuing to follow our process, we applied our evaluation levers to the four problem areas. Once again, the levers were discussed as part of the collaborative process, and once again evaluation appeared as a part (rather than a primary focus) of the overarching coaching and training programme, assumed to be conducted sometime after its completion. A summary of the key levers is presented below as a frame to help design the form and process of evaluation.

Figure 21: Evaluation levers

Original evaluation lever	Evaluation lever in this context
Primary goal	Productivity and well-being, in terms of individual responsibility for self-management and a shared responsibility for collective management.
Evaluation status	Formal evaluation which is external, impartial and independent and, at the same time, collaborative and supportive. Towards shared responsibility for each other's well-being (rather than judgement, conflict, and blame based).
Multigenerational leadership pools	An approach which is creative/imaginative to enable a team with diverse backgrounds to contribute. Moving beyond the ability to clearly articulate words, to an approach that supports and encourages people to articulate potentially sensitive well-being aspects of their experience.
Organizational context	An historical approach focusing on productivity, but a renewed emphasis on improvement in broader terms – i.e. moving forwards in terms of productivity with well-being at the heart of that improvement. This is based on a context where individual contributions are revealed and valued, towards a greater collective appreciation of the leadership team's influence on the whole organization.

Table 40   The context for evaluation

Problem area	Evaluation lever	Ambidextrous leadership and coaching focus
Data usage	Primary goal	Productivity balanced with well-being Personal responsibility/outcomes balanced with collective responsibility/outcomes
Dissemination	Evaluation status	External impartiality balanced with internal emotional commitment
Timelines	Multigenerational leadership pools	Well-articulated outcomes/impacts balanced with elicited/fuzzier outcomes/impacts Historical impacts balanced with future-paced intended impacts
Competency	Organizational context	Existing capabilities balanced with developmental, capacity-building outcomes for future evaluation

When the evaluation levers are applied to the four problem areas, Table 40 emerged as a representation of the evaluation environment.

Exploring and clarifying the evaluation environment was useful and remained an important part of the wider cultural and strategic dimensions of leadership coaching evaluation, even though the coaching was part of a wider set of activity to be evaluated. The process clearly highlighted certain values that were important to the overall strategic direction of a team, but balanced the shorter-term operational and mechanical aspects of evaluation, the longer-term direction of the leadership team and the developmental fuzziness of taking a creative approach. We found useful comparisons (through the different approaches) with the case study in Chapter 8, where the organization was insistent that the evaluation of hard targets needed to be carried out in a psychologically informed environment with servant-hearted leaders.

As with all our case studies, this table was refined through the collaborative process to provide a clear frame for a shared understanding and agreement of the particular approach to evaluation.

The design experience

With no existing (explicit) leadership structure or strategy chain to work with, we once again saw evaluation as a conductor of an orchestra, focused on intangibles such as tone, tempo and volume. This viewpoint echoes the last case study, where a less formal, collaborative and emergent approach to outcomes was more appropriate to a structured, goal-setting approach, followed by systematic, formal data collection.

Where the evaluation model might fit

In this case, we positioned evaluation at the end of the coaching and training process. However, our approach was to align eventual evaluation data at an early stage by scoping leader's action plans to embed positive changes for future behavioural and well-being outcomes, as well as impact on wider organizational structures and systems.

An inventory of needs

As we continue to follow our sequence of evaluation theory events, an inventory of needs facilitated the practical design for a system to be workable for the unique internal context of the organization. The inventory of needs in this case is a direct response to the leadership team's own recognition of what we might typically call 'blind spots', but, as with the last case study, were framed more as opportunities.

Table 41 Using evaluation levers to reveal an inventory of needs to exploit opportunities

Evaluation lever	Definition	Opportunity (partly recognized from within the internal context)	Inventory of needs (to exploit opportunities)
Primary goal	Embedding well-being in productivity improvement	Balanced approach for longer-term resilience and sustainability	Evidence of impact on well-being and productivity
Evaluation status	Augmenting what is already informally known – in terms of process and credibility of outcomes	Opportunity for development and recognition of achievement	A level of externality (impartiality) but emotionally supportive
Multigenerational	Enabling diverse backgrounds and characteristics to express themselves and engage	Empowerment and development of groups to share voice	Creative, expressive and engaging
Organizational context	Developing leadership team-based culture, and commitment to further development	Capacity-building for balancing historical improvements and motivation for future improvements	Collaborative, open-ended review of past achievements to inform forward-looking approach to embedding learning and successes

In this way, the inventory again shifted from its original design modus operandi towards a strategic function closer to an organizational development cycle. The final column provides a summary of the strategic insight which had not yet been articulated to, or expressed by, the leadership team or organization, crystallizing a set of parameters for the design of the framework. As we noticed in the last case study, the inventory framework can be used as an organic, emergent process for dialogue and discussion, and informing the practical design of the evaluation model.

The evaluation experience

Unlike the other cases, the inventory of needs highlighted a real requirement for openness to enable the leadership team, who had experienced the coaching and training, to feel they could express *their* voice, and the learning *they* had attained, as a strong motivator to encourage commitment to future improvement. Within this context, it can be seen that the particular evaluation approach was in itself a strategic reorientation of the leadership team towards ambidexterity, that is, it was an attempt to rebalance a prior (unhealthy) focus on productivity targets to new ways of working at the organizational level, where productivity was integrated with well-being. There was recognition that, by establishing this among the leadership team, this could help the cascade across the wider organization, through leaders, to operational staff at all other levels.

Table 42 is the resultant, intentionally open, ambidextrous framework. This was not explicitly discussed and agreed, but did underpin the design of the framework for the evaluation team. It was particularly important to establish clarity around this, given the focus of the coaching and training programme was delivered by another external organization. While this was not something the evaluators could influence, it was important to establish the role of it in the chain of logic for the evaluation.

Table 42 Evaluation framework

Subordinate strategy for primary goal	Exploitative leadership targets	Explorative leadership targets	Leadership coaching focus	Evaluation criteria	Strategic data
Employee well-being as a driver of productivity	Productivity improvement (as defined by leaders)	Well-being improvement (as defined by leaders)	Commitment to balancing the achievement of productivity and well-being improvement	Self-reporting Peer accountability Collective accountability	Themes generated from: self-reporting, peer accountability, collective accountability

Evaluation workshops

The practical design of the evaluation, therefore, centred around holding interactive workshops with different groups of leaders that had participated in the coaching and training programme (senior leaders, middle leaders and team leaders for different service areas within Middleshire). The workshops invited participants to reflect on:

- the most significant changes, outcomes and/or impacts they experienced
- the most significant 'ripple effects' of those impacts on others' lives
- any actions to embed the positive effects in their own workplace, including their own work
- how to disseminate these effects for others in their organization and beyond.

The workshops were intentionally open without further specific focus, to enable the leaders to express their own voice.

This was an approach inspired by the long-standing, inclusive and participatory 'Most Significant Change' technique, where the thoughts and experiences of participants take precedence over predefined outcomes by others. However, other aspects were integrated, including appreciative inquiry (an approach focusing on the more positive experiences to motivate buy-in to future improvement states), and organizational play, encouraging an informal playful atmosphere where people can openly share new, creative and imaginative ideas and innovations.

As such, participants were invited to prepare for the event by bringing objects, images, pieces of text or work (their own or others') which represented their most significant changes/outcomes/impacts since being part of the coaching and training programme. During the workshops, the evaluators encouraged the sharing of stories around the objects to help explore their impact, and then use these as prompts about how to embed the positive results. This included sharing ideas about what else they could do as leaders to build even more positive change moving forward, what their teams could do, what the wider organization could do, and what their wider communities could do.

Impact points

In line with the framework below, it was important to capture individual changes (to express and value unique leader perspective) as well as team changes (to encourage the aspect of shared responsibility and accountability for productivity and well-being). In its own way, this distinction acts as a weighting mechanism for the evaluation assessment.

Table 43 below summarizes **individual** impacts:

Table 43   Individual impacts

	Productivity	Well-being
Self-awareness of own predispositions, values, beliefs and behaviours; their impact on their own self-care, and impact on service delivery and others' well-being and productivity.	+	+
Increased 'noticing' capabilities, and recognition of the need to spend effort to reflect/adjust in relation to self-care and well-being – and the impact on others.	+	+
New self-care practices linked to work–life balance, especially 'embedded every day', and the role of this in enhancing practice and re-energizing.	+	+

(Continued)

Table 43   (Continued)

	Productivity	Well-being
Advanced workload prioritization skills, including the importance of the timing of responding to work activity, as well as broader awareness of the wider impacts of these on wider team resilience, team well-being and service delivery/performance.	+	+
Responsibility for changing own behavioural patterns and differentiating between what can be changed, what might need more change-effort, and what cannot be changed.	+	+
Greater appreciation of own health and well-being, and how to positively affect it – for example, healthier eating, physical activity, purposeful breathing activity.	+	+
Developed strategies and tactics to create positive, engaging and rewarding working environments (e.g. positive conversations, play and time out, creating everyday opportunities for learning) and awareness of broader impacts on team well-being, performance and service delivery.	+	+
Increased emotional intelligence, specifically in relation to awareness of personal impact on others.	+	+
Increased connectedness, empathy and understanding among the teams.	+	+

The list below summarizes **team** impacts:

- Increased transparency as a team.
- Fit together as a team.
- Manage negative voices.
- Become more open.
- Increased awareness of each other.
- Increased adhesion/bond together.
- Completing tasks that we need to deliver.
- Being allowed to be ourselves.
- Increased trust.
- Legitimizing 'time out' – to re-energize and be better able to manage multiple pressures.
- Knowing how to prioritize workloads including how and when to say 'no'.

- Managing resilience and well-being through intentionally using positive thinking and reframing.
- Purposefully managing own emotions with and for others.

The final part of the workshops focused on an emergent vision to make well-being an everyday thing, which could be delivered though:

- Recognition boards – as part of a wider recognition and reward strategy.
- An employee charter which specifies values and behaviours (embedding well-being across the organization).
- Smile: have you made anyone smile today?
- Encourage Fruit Fridays.
- Enable learning in new ways.
- Need to spread through teams first – six key messages.
- Needs to be kept simple.
- Send regular emails/keep communications going.

The workshop also identified some wider priorities for systemic change in the broader organization:

- Communicating achievements, successes, good practices, and any policy-level changes.
- Adapt the organization as well as self and the team.
- Keep developing and make the change 'happen every day'.
- Involve, share, and make the change together.
- Creating positive working environments where 'small' actions create a positive and engaging atmosphere (e.g. smiling, praising, recognizing achievements, 'new face' welcomes, supporting in one-to-one and team contexts).
- Promoting learning and cross-departmental empathy and awareness through a team leadership forum, 'back-to-the-floor', job-shadowing, and/or 'show-and-tell' opportunities.
- Promoting learning related to resilience and well-being (e.g. tips of the day, message of the day, internal courses).

Final thoughts

This final case study differs from its predecessors, specifically by relating the experiences of an evaluation practitioner, detached and outside the realm of the organization's leadership training programme. It also focuses on a new dimension for evaluation as a driver of impact and change. As such, it does not provide the structure (flowcharts, calculation tables, etc.) of evaluation as part of an integrated coaching process focused on RoI and adopts slightly different methodologies to achieve evaluation data (e.g. participatory workshops to elicit data). These differences may be down to the evaluator's perspective (outside looking in), but the fundamental principles of becoming immersed in the internal context, the usefulness of tools and the illuminating powers of ambidexterity, remain and allow the evaluator to achieve their goal – proving the transferability of the system across, not only diverse organizations, but evaluator professional perspectives.

In particular, this case illustrated the applicability and utilization of an ambidextrous approach to the evaluation when it is part of a wider set of activities. It highlighted how ambidexterity could be used to implicitly inform and shape the design of evaluation, in a way which was aligned to broader strategic direction and intent of an organization, despite not having explicit strategic goals or targets. Indeed, this is a context where, having explicit goals and outcomes, in addition to the institutional productivity targets and goals, could be destructive to the wider intent of balancing productivity with well-being. This evidences the idea that the act of evaluation – and the practical mechanics of how it is done – can positively influence that which is measured; in this case, it was the ambidextrous balance of productivity and well-being, via enabling the voice and imagination of a group of leaders under pressure.

The approach discussed is a bold and unorthodox one, especially in a context where statistics related to targets are paramount. In each application, it is clear that there is an associated leader who commissions the open and creative process and is willing and able to implement the actions sometime after the evaluation report is produced. Perhaps this is because it aligns with their personal leadership style and values, and because they have the positional power to enact the collaborative plans created. While the approach has created a legacy of impact effects within the organizations adopting it, it is also a possibility that it would not appeal to a more directive or autocratic leadership style or set of values. There is also the possibility that the commissioning leader may not have the power or resource to implement the co-created action plans and, along with the evaluation team, must be aware of this risk and be prepared to respond to it – especially if they want to release the motivational power of such forms of leadership coaching evaluation.

11 Conclusion – Looking forward: highlights and lingering doubts

Introduction

We have achieved what we set out to do: to write a guidebook for professionals providing a practical way to evaluate the impact of leadership coaching, accompanied by a compelling argument about why it matters. We have also gone beyond our initial expectations in producing a system that is not only transferable but agile enough to produce evaluation data, when called upon, for areas of leadership with low financial legitimacy but highly relevant at this time, such as well-being, behaviours and potential. Widening the scope for evaluation in this way has successfully expanded the purview of leadership and what defines a leader in this current environment. In this final chapter we look forward, developing insights we gained during the writing of this book, conceptualizing some of the highlights and challenges, providing some last-minute tips, and a glimpse of the future for evaluation in an ever more dynamic context.

Reflecting on our experiences

Highlights – what we wanted to achieve (and more)

Simply put, we wanted to achieve credibility with our reader by presenting a practical evaluation theory that was relevant, relatable and accessible. Equally as important, we wanted to get professionals to take evaluation seriously and, to do so, we set out to provide a compelling argument, using a simple workable organizational function to produce high-level strategic data at very little cost, but of great value. In the first instance, we were pleased that our theory worked in practice but, as we reflected on what we had achieved, it was the unexpected add-ons that truly defined our model, of which there were three particular highlights: transferability, strategic value and diverse return on investment.

- **Transferability**

One of our significant challenges was to prove the transferability of our system. As an antidote to previous research projects and criticism of narrow focus and one-dimensionality, we deliberately wanted to explore across different organizational sectors. At the time, we were satisfied that if we could prove our model was applicable to diverse sector primary goals (profit, performance and purpose), that would be sufficient evidence of transferability. However, as our confidence grew, we became increasingly ambitious, as evinced by our case study in Chapter 9 where we successfully applied our model to a pioneering leadership coaching programme for schools. Serendipitously, the adaptability of our model provided us with a number of fascinating insights, beyond the usual compare and contrast learning we would have expected, which added to our knowledge. As we progressed, transferability became synonymous with sector differences, and we have chosen four focal points for learning that we felt were of particular interest to evaluators:

1 The strategic continuum for evaluation needs

What we began to notice was that the sector primary goal dictates the evaluation system design, specifically with regard to the process to produce an inventory of needs. In essence, the more the sector primary goal was singularly focused on financial performance for profit or accountability, the more operational (focused on practicalities) their design needs were, for competency (collection of data), consistency (dissemination of data) and legitimization (explanation of data).

Therefore, when we formulated an inventory of needs for a school's evaluation framework (Chapter 9), we were initially sceptical about its usefulness or its necessity. However, in going through with the process, we found that the inventory of needs evolved naturally and that the 'needs' column of the framework was far more strategically focused than in a conventional private, public or third sector setting. In fact, what we found was that, where there are multiple stakeholders and ambiguous leadership outcomes, the inventory of needs becomes an initial indicator for the destination of strategic data.

We came to visualize this as a continuum with exploitative financially dominant targets at one end, eliciting operational needs, and multilayered leadership goals and behaviours with little financial motivation at the other end, from which emerged strategic opportunities. This knowledge was to become a useful tool for us at the early stages of designing an organization's evaluation system, providing a simple rule of thumb to set our expectations and allow us to anticipate the direction of travel for evaluation.

2 One sector's challenge is another's opportunity

Leading on from the previous section, this insight continues to develop the notion that unstructured explorative leadership contexts provide the low-hanging strategic fruit for the evaluator. Again, our examples in Chapter 9 (chosen as an evaluation extreme) and Chapter 10, redefined other organizations' challenges to be solved, as opportunities to be exploited. Thematically, this lack of structure or direction in the organization was considered, at face value, to be a potential headache for the evaluator. In reality, the opposite was true and, once the practitioner had managed the concept of evaluation in an unstructured environment, it became a key to a rich vein of strategic data. Clearly, this might reflect a complete absence of existing data or strategic leadership direction (where there is a void to be filled); however, as with our 'needs continuum', those organizations with established leadership strategies were found to be focused on finding answers to challenges to evaluation, whereas those organizations at the other end of the continuum were tasked with exploiting these (challenges) as potential opportunities that fed into the wider strategy.

3 Diverse definitions of ambidexterity

For the purposes of evaluation, specifically the retrieval of strategic data, different definitions of ambidexterity were to be expected; however, at another level, ambidexterity was a constant companion to us throughout our journeys exploring the organizational internal context. Here we found ambidextrous perspectives defined the individual organization, and were the key to understanding how the organization operates and to forging an effective collaborative relationship. The idea for the evaluator is that they take a wider view of ambidexterity and do not ignore those tensions that do not directly apply to leadership, coaching or evaluation, as they are vital clues to the organizational DNA and help shape the design of any evaluation system.

4 Steep and shallow leadership hierarchies

Another key indicator for the evaluator is the organization's leadership hierarchies. These generally fell into two categories: steep (multiple layers of

Figure 22: Some implications of the characteristics of steep and shallow leadership hierarchies by sector, of which the evaluator should be aware

Sector	Steep leadership hierarchy	Shallow leadership hierarchy
Public	Overly structured career paths that overlook individual leadership talent	N/A
	Leadership expectations for frontline staff that go unrecognized	N/A
Third	Blanket leadership development programmes	Dominant CEO
	Indiscriminate targets for promotion that do not recognize outstanding performance	N/A
Private sector	Meaningless layers of middle management	Dominant CEO
	Lack of discrimination at lower levels between career pathways and outstanding performance	Subjective and discretionary judgements
	Too many leadership posts devaluing promotions	Limited opportunities for promotion Succession issues

management or leadership responsibilities at all levels of the organization); or shallow (few layers of leadership or a dominant senior leadership team). We found that unique leadership hierarchies had significant implications for the practitioner, and an understanding of these gave the evaluator an aura of expertise in the eyes of the client.

These four focal points are not exhaustive of the unexpected learning from the process and they are indicative of the continuous acquisition of knowledge from which the evaluator should expect to benefit as they develop their practice. At this stage they are presented as tips, providing an extra dimension of expertise to the design of any system. In essence, having an eye for unexpected details, and knowing where to look for them, acts as a spotlight to help the evaluator read the organization.

- **Strategic value**

The data we retrieved from our evaluation system, without exception, was of high strategic value. One of the main reasons for this was that the evaluation process seemed to naturally fall into two parts: for accountability and information. As the strategic focus came at the end of the programme, this presented the opportunity for strategic targets to evolve as part of the process. In other words, the scope of the strategy to be informed was unrestricted. This meant that the organization was constantly surprised by data that informed unexpected areas of their wider strategy, to accompany those areas where they had requested or anticipated data.

On this basis, we would recommend that the evaluator is ever watchful for nuggets of data thrown up during the evaluation process, and keeps a record of these (or regularly discusses them with the collaboration group) as potential additional destinations for dissemination at the end of the programme, to make the most of evaluation as a strategic opportunity.

- **Diverse return on investment**

Perhaps the most significant surprising outcome was the adaptability of our theory to produce diverse RoI. As previously stated, when we set out we would have been satisfied by proving that our model was transferable across the three main sectors we researched. In terms of transferability, our initial challenge was to ensure that the model could be adapted to suit the internal contexts of different sectors to be workable; however, when we considered the second part of the evaluation equation, the retrieval and dissemination of useful strategic data, we found that our model had the capacity to zero in on specific (unconventional) evaluation foci aligned to different primary goals.

We expected to be able to produce a credible financial RoI, but what we did not expect was that we could also report on other less tangible RoI targets. The agility we had built into our model enabled us to not only respond to the organization's needs, but to produce a relevant RoI when called upon. We found we were able to build in a specific focus for a final evaluation figure, informed by the collaborative process, that was highly relevant to the individual organization, outside the traditional realm of RoI. In other words, all the client had to do was tell us what they wanted measuring and in what currency.

For instance, in the second case study (Chapter 8), the client makes clear at the beginning of the collaboration that 'behavioural RoI' is the significant, relevant target for evaluation. Accordingly, we were able to anticipate the direction of travel of resultant strategic data at an early stage. In contrast, our most ambitious case study (Chapter 9) illustrates an organization that is unclear about specific targets for RoI, and it is not until near the end of the programme that we are able to fashion our bottom-line reporting to focus on RoI for *potential*. In the final case study (Chapter 10) we have managed to build in an RoI element to include well-being as part of the organization's primary goal.

Essentially, we have managed to leave behind the ongoing debate around evaluation about the relevance of financial RoI, moving it on to the more diverse bottom-line outcomes that currently define the leadership environment. In this model we have effectively used evaluation to redefine RoI, opening up the scope of any return on investment to include hitherto nebulous or ambiguous desired goals, such as behaviours, potential and well-being, giving them a platform for credible tangible assessment.

The reasons professionals will continue to find evaluation difficult in the future

We have explored the evaluation conundrum in detail. We have identified, refined and provided new perspectives on the challenging environment for evaluation, even managing to harness some of these ideas as tools or promising movements. We have also examined the subtext for evaluation, the will to evaluate, and now have an acute awareness of the intellectual as well as the practical barriers we face. This new knowledge has enabled us to produce the model we hoped for, but it has also exposed faultlines in the system (in the widest sense) that we have no way of controlling. Accordingly, it would be naive of us, and we would be underserving our reader, if we were not to share some lingering doubts, amid the fanfare of our achievements, about evaluation as a persistent thorn in the organizational side. We have encapsulated these doubts in three categories that the practitioner should be aware of – areas of concern that, despite the answers we have produced in this book, are unlikely to conveniently disappear: the exponential gap, the internal context and the evaluator mindset.

1 The exponential gap

Throughout this book we have referred to the different speeds at which the operating environment, leadership (development) and evaluation of impact have evolved. We have concluded that organizations have successfully responded to external forces beyond their control by running leadership strategies in tandem, or pretty close, to produce strategies to survive or thrive. At the same time, evaluation appears as an also-ran. This understanding has been critical to our work, explaining the importance of analysing the receptiveness of the unique evaluation environment for each organization, as the basis for formulating a workable system. It is also clear to us that the pace of change is likely to accelerate, exacerbating this problem in the future for evaluators. We have named this particular phenomenon the exponential gap.

The exponential age is a phrase most recently coined by technological analyst Azeem Azhar (2021), describing the problem of rapidly accelerating technological change in a society evolving at a more gradual, incremental pace. We have drawn on parallels from this idea and adapted it as an elegant description of the gulf between leadership development and evaluation. Interestingly, Azhar orients his thinking (to narrow the gap) around the need for technology to be restored to a position of service, where society decides what outcomes it wants from the technology it develops. Similarly, we see evaluation as potentially managing the dynamic world of leadership and the growth of coaching, clarifying targets that are constantly moving and holding coaches to account for the currency of their interventions.

We would argue that, unless we manage the exponential gap which is naturally set to widen, by making a concerted effort to develop our evaluation techniques, it will disrupt the evaluation environment which will be less receptive to our ideas.

2 The internal context: how organizations respond to catastrophes

One of the major sources of the exponential gap is the way organizations respond to external forces. We have evidenced that organizations are strategically creative in the face of contingencies outside their control and that these should no longer be considered problematic to evaluation. However, it is the subsequent knock-on effect to the internal context that evaluators should now be aware of, and, as strategists become increasingly inventive, the internal context is liable to become ever more complex.

A traumatic disruption like the Covid-19 pandemic, for instance, provides the organization with an opportunity to flex its strategic grey matter to come up with innovative and resourceful ideas to survive a crisis. This resourcefulness is not in question, despite the ensuing chaos of the event. However, it is the resultant internal context for leadership that will now tax the evaluator. As organizations realign to flexible working hours, renewed well-being and mental health agendas, different styles of communication, etc., there is no doubt that leadership strategies will keep in step, while coaching races to keep up and evaluation is in danger of falling further behind. We are confident that our evaluation model will equip the practitioner to cope with a dramatic and rapidly changing internal context; however, the evaluator should be wary of the repercussions of such a state of flux and accept this as a new-normal leadership environment.

3 The evaluator mindset

We accept that our case studies are illustrative examples of our system in action, emerging from established relationships with the organizations; therefore, it is sensible to assume that the evaluator will not always work in such a receptive context. Accordingly, there is every possibility that the efforts needed to convince the client to place evaluation higher up the executive agenda are far more strenuous, and the extra burden of having to sell evaluation may just tempt the evaluator to acquiesce to the client's lack of motivation or interest. This possible scenario characterizes the nascent stage for evaluation, placing the enthusiastic evaluator twixt and tween the less than enthusiastic client: the converted and the unconverted. Here, the evaluator has a choice between 'the customer is always right' and, now knowing the implications of overlooking evaluation, standing their ground.

Our assertion is that evaluation serves many masters and is here to stay, and, although it is not a mandatory part of the coaching contract, practitioners would do well to anticipate its growing influence. This book focuses on evaluation as having two capabilities, for accountability and strategic data; but in the future, we can also envisage evaluation as defining the coach offering, providing a Kitemark for quality assurance as the client picks their way through an increasingly crowded marketplace for leadership coaching. For the time being, we would urge the evaluator not to be tempted by shortcuts, on the basis that the client might be none the wiser, but to promote evaluation as a vital new dimension of coaching (for which they should expect to get paid).

Practically speaking

Finally, we wanted to highlight a few of the practical issues that evaluators should not just assume they will overcome, but may need to develop their own specific strategies to move forward effectively. This concluding section also satisfies our commitment to closing the gap between theory and practice, covering the niggling contingencies we found ourselves referring to as – 'Yes, but what if…?'

First contingency – How easy will it be to collaborate?

We have emphasized throughout this book that we believe an effective collaborative relationship is essential to evaluation. In all of our case studies we have reported on an existing relationship with the client, where a collaborative environment, defined by trust, domain reputation (the coach evaluator) and a mutually beneficial end goal, has either been in place or has been easily forged. We would urge our readers to expect, instead, that most collaborative relationships of this nature will be started from scratch as part of a wider leadership coaching proposal. From this perspective, the inevitable question is: how open to collaboration is my client?

Assuming that you are a coach reading this book, we would imagine you are well-versed in forming a working relationship with a sponsor or stakeholder, and an organizational evaluator will already have access to the internal context. However, beyond coaching behaviours and internal familiarity, we have selected three practical tips that we picked up along the way to support a collaborative relationship.

- **Conquer the internal context**

Enough has been said about the internal context. However, what bears repeating is that the evaluator should see time spent understanding the idiosyncrasies and machinations of their client as an investment. Without an understanding of, or access to, the leadership structures, needs, culture, values, drivers, insecurities, contradictions, tensions, etc. (the list is endless) of the organization, any evaluation process is half-hearted. In essence, this book is irrelevant without the evaluator conquering the internal context.

We also saw in our third case study (Chapter 9) the temptation to shortcut the process, where there were areas of our theory that, at first glance, seemingly did not apply to the situation. Using the agility of our model the process was easily adapted and our efforts to explore the internal context paid dividends, opening up new dimensions of understanding and unexpected strategic areas to which we could steer emergent data. Accordingly, conquering the internal context is an essential to building a simpatico collaborative relationship.

- **Learn to speak the language**

The language of evaluation is something the practitioner should not underestimate. The way we communicate as evaluators is highly relevant on two levels: relatability and sensitivity.

Earlier on, we documented how the language of ambidexterity was an entry point to the organizational mindset, as a series of carefully worded propositions and tensions that were both familiar and relatable. The evaluator should bear in mind the effectiveness of language when building a collaborative relationship, identifying coaching targets and leadership outcomes, and adapting when transitioning from one sector client to another. The ability to speak the language of the client is a powerful tool for the evaluator and should be considered in the same vein as other coaching tools (empathy, rapport, etc.) used to forge working relationships.

In our four case studies there are examples of language, deliberately designed to be sensitive to the stakeholder and the coachee. In Chapter 10 we describe this as a new, expected competency to maintain and not undermine the positive tone of the overall coaching. Similarly, in Chapter 8 focused on the third sector, the evaluator goes to great lengths to consider the possible reaction of the leadership coachee, when designated their particular weighting classification (improved, maintained, excelled), to avoid any negative connotations or implications of criticisms of attitude.

In all cases, language is a key to unlock the collaborative relationship and build a positive environment of trust; it also contributes to the smooth transference of evaluation across sectors, and one needs only to compare and contrast the language used in Chapter 7 (private sector) and the case study in Chapter 9 (school) to see two examples of how the evaluator can use language in the design of a relatable framework.

- **Master the art of difficult conversations**

One of our claims is that the external evaluator can act as a quasi-consultant or wise person to the organization, and an arbiter of outcomes, judgements and the dissemination of data. This of course relies on the evaluator's ability to become a trusted part of the organization, in order to intervene at various levels of the leadership hierarchy over potential areas of conflict, contradiction and bias.

We imagine that the coach evaluator is skilled at the art of diplomacy (difficult conversations) as part of their overarching job; however, their intervention might also require the organizational executive to act on sensitive or controversial recommendations, specifically in the area of busting silos and tendentious motivations of evaluation stakeholders. The success or not of an evaluation programme, as with all coaching engagements, depends on the honesty of a relationship where a safe environment to challenge and ask provocative questions is essential.

Second contingency – Can I (we) spare the time?

- **An investment in time**

In coaching parlance, we talk about time management in terms of making judgement calls by prioritizing important over urgent work. This same technique applies to evaluation. It has been our intention throughout this book to present a compelling argument for evaluation as an important strategic tool, claiming that to ignore it is tantamount to negligence. However, we are also acutely aware that leaders at all levels, in all sectors, are time poor, and the onus will often fall on the evaluator to sell the concept of evaluation as an important strategic component with priority over urgent business imperatives. Similarly, having read our book, following our processes to the letter, the coach may highlight their own challenging time commitments. Accordingly, we felt it would not be good enough for us to promote evaluation sanctimoniously as an investment, and we were conscious that the evaluator would probably require more practical motivations to commit the time and effort to our process. We have two such motivations to offer you:

1 It gets quicker over time – not only in the execution and formulation process with any new client, but with existing clients once a programme has been bedded in.

2   Charge for your time – a major part of the collaborative process involves one-to-ones with the coachee as a version of introductory, chemistry and debrief meetings. Furthermore, evaluation is now an integral part of the coach offering providing a valuable second (to actual coaching outcomes) service which, positioned in this way, should not be difficult to sell.

• **The danger of collaboration overload**

There is currently a school of thought that has warned of the negative effects of collaborative overload (Cross et al. 2021). Figures from this research claim that (partially down to the increase in remote communication) collaborative work has risen by 50 per cent and accounts for 85 per cent of the average leader's week. This is a counter-intuitive idea (to our theory) but it is well worth mentioning here, to remind the evaluator not to take for granted, or abuse, the attention span of the organizational executive.

At the end of each case study (except Chapter 10), we have been careful to produce an assessment of the time and effort that went into the evaluation process for that organization: who was involved and how many hours they contributed. With this in mind, the evaluator is in a much better position to set some ground rules for the client, managing expectations of required commitment and crystallizing the level of contribution that the organization is willing and able to sign up to.

The evaluator's own ambidextrous tension

This is our final challenge to the coach evaluator. At the outset of this book, we acknowledged that leadership coaching is a business and, like any business, there is an ambidextrous tension between short-term financial gain and long-term values-driven goals. We have used a series of provocations to stimulate this debate for coaches, calling into question the integrity and effectiveness of any coaching relationship that chooses to ignore evaluation in the context we have laid out here. In the end, it is for the coach to make the decision.

Our previous research with coaches revealed very different attitudes to evaluation, ranging from casual to high-level scrutiny of RoI for self-serving purposes. In this book we have shifted the focus for evaluation and it has now become a meaningful part of the coach contract. As with the organizations we have worked with, the coach may choose to view their own ambidextrous tensions in terms of the sectors they are serving at the time, along with their own coaching motivations.

In any case, we present evaluation as an opportunity for the coach to increase their value to the organization, raising the professional profile of coaching by contributing a structured and sophisticated understanding of the client's unique needs, dispelling the raised eyebrows of executive cynics and rewarding the faith of long-term leadership strategists (not to mention the significant sums invested).

In time, we predict that evaluation will be an essential part of the coach offering, and organizations will come to expect a slick and effective approach from their providers as part of their overarching leadership strategy. We also predict that coaching, as a business, will continue to grow at pace and evaluation will become a defining factor for coach advocacy in an increasingly crowded marketplace.

We began this piece of work asking questions of evaluation: whether it is workable and what contribution it could make that would encourage practitioners to take notice. We end by posing a new question: in this new world of leadership can we afford not to place the evaluation of the impact of leadership coaching at the top of the executive agenda?

References

Adair, J. G. (1984) The Hawthorne effect: A reconsideration of the methodological arti-fact, *Journal of Applied Psychology*, 69(2): 334–45. https://doi.org/10.1037/0021-9010.69.2.334

Angrave, D., Charlwood, A., Kirkpatrick, I., Lawrence, M. and Stuart, M. (2016) HR and analytics: Why HR is set to fail the big data challenge, *Human Resource Management Journal*, 26(1): 1–11.

Azhar, A. (2021) *Exponential: How Accelerating Technology Is Leaving Us Behind and What to Do About It.* London: Cornerstone.

Becker, B., Huselid, M. and Beatty, R. (2009) *The Differentiated Workforce: Transform-ing Talent into Strategic Impact.* Boston, MA: Harvard Business School Press.

Beer, M. (2015) HRM at a crossroads: Comments on 'Evolution of Strategic HRM Through Two Founding Books: A 30th Anniversary Perspective on Development of the Field', *Human Resource Management*, 54(3): 417–21.

Cappelli, P. (2008) Talent management for the twenty-first century, *Harvard Business Review*, 86(3): 74–81.

CIPD (2008) *Annual Survey Report: Learning and Development 2008*, Reference 4321. London: Chartered Institute of Personnel and Development.

CIPD (2011) *The Coaching Climate*, Reference 5629. London: Chartered Institute of Per-sonnel and Development.

CIPD (2013) *Annual Survey Report: Learning and Development 2013*, Reference 6174. London: Chartered Institute of Personnel and Development.

CIPD (2014) *Annual Survey Report: Learning and Development 2014*, Reference 6477. London: Chartered Institute of Personnel and Development.

CIPD (2015) *Annual Survey Report: Learning and Development 2015*, Reference 6942. London: Chartered Institute of Personnel and Development.

CIPD (2017) *HR Outlook*, Reference 7437. London: Chartered Institute of Personnel and Development.

CIPD (2018) *Over-Skilled and Underused: Investigating the Untapped Potential of UK Skills*, Reference 7757. London: Chartered Institute of Personnel and Development.

CIPD (2020) *Learning and Skills at Work*, Reference 8018. London: Chartered Institute of Personnel and Development.

Collins, J. (2005) Level 5 leadership: The triumph of humility and fierce resolve, *Harvard Business Review* magazine, July, p. 13. Available at: https://hbr.org/2005/07/level-5-leadership-the-triumph-of-humility-and-fierce-resolve [accessed 14 January 2022].

Cross, R., Benson, M., Kostal, J. and Milnor, R.J. (2021) Collaboration overload is sinking productivity, *Harvard Business Review* magazine, 7 September. Available at: https://hbr.org/2021/09/collaboration-overload-is-sinking-productivity [accessed 14 January 2022].

DDI (2018) *Global Leadership Forecast 2018*. Available at: https://www.ddiworld.com/research/global-leadership-forecast-2018 [accessed 14 January 2022].

Ely, K., Boyce, L., Nelson, J., Zaccaro, S., Hernez-Broome, G. and Whyman, W. (2010) Evaluating leadership coaching: A review and integrated framework, *Leadership Quarterly*, 21(4): 585–99.

Ericksen, J. and Dyer, L. (2005) Toward a strategic human resource management model of high reliability organisation performance, *International Journal of Human Resource Management*, 16(6): 907–28.

Fernandez-Araoz, C., Groysberg, B. and Nohria, N. (2011) How to hang on to your high potentials, *Harvard Business Review* magazine, October, pp. 76–83. Available at: https://hbr.org/2011/10/how-to-hang-on-to-your-high-potentials [accessed 14 January 2022].

Gallup (2016) *How Millennials Want to Work and Live*. Washington, DC: Gallup Inc.

Hall, D., Otazo, K. and Hollenbeck, G. (1999) Behind closed doors: What really happens in executive coaching, *Organisational Dynamics*, 27(3): 39–53.

Hatum, A. (2010). *Next Generation Talent Management: Talent Management to Survive Turmoil*. New York: Palgrave Macmillan.

ICF in partnership with the Human Capital Institute (2014) *Building a Coaching Culture*. Available at: http://coachfederation.org/about/landing.cfm?ItemNumber=3674 [accessed 14 January 2022].

Jamieson, M., Wall, T. and Moore, N. (2020) Why evaluation of leadership coaching counts, *International Journal of Evidence Based Coaching & Mentoring*, S14: 3–18. DOI: 10.24384/prb0-s320.

Kaufman, B. (2015) The RBV theory foundation of strategic HRM: Critical flaws, problems for research and practice, and an alternative economics paradigm, *Human Resource Management Journal*, 25(4): 516–40.

Kirkpatrick, D. (1959a) Techniques for evaluation programs, *Journal of the American Society of Training Directors*, 13(11): 3–9.

Kirkpatrick, D. (1959b) Techniques for evaluation programs – Part 2: Learning, *Journal of the American Society of Training Directors*, 13(12): 21–6.

Lepak, D. and Shaw, J. (2008) Strategic HRM in North America: Looking to the future, *International Journal of Human Resource Management*, 19(8): 1486–99.

Lewis, R. and Heckman, R. (2006) Talent management: A critical review, *Human Resource Management Review*, 16(2): 139–54.

March, J. (1991) Exploration and exploitation in organisational learning, *Organisation Science*, 2(1): 71–87.

Maslow, A.H. (1998) *Maslow on Management*. New York: John Wiley & Sons.

McDonnell, A. (2011) Still fighting the 'war for talent'? Bridging the science versus practice gap, *Journal of Business and Psychology*, 26(2): 169–73. Available at: https://www.jstor.org/stable/41474865 [accessed 14 January 2022].

Michaels, E., Handfield-Jones, H. and Axelrod, B. (2001) *The War for Talent*. Boston, MA: Harvard Business School Press.

O'Reilly, C. and Tushman, M. (2004) The ambidextrous organisation, *Harvard Business Review* magazine, April, pp. 74–83. Available at: https://hbr.org/2004/04/the-ambidextrous-organization [accessed 14 January 2022].

O'Reilly, C. and Tushman, M. (2013) *Organisational Ambidexterity: Past, Present and Future*, Research Paper No. 2130. Stanford Research Paper Series.

Phillips, J. (1994) Measuring ROI in an established program, in J. Phillips (ed.) *In Action: Measuring Return on Investment*, Vol. 1. Alexandria, VA: American Society for Training and Development, pp. 187–97.

Prokopeak, M. (2018) *Follow the Leader(ship) Spending*, Chief Learning Officer Business Intelligence Board website. Available at: https://www.chieflearningofficer.com/2018/03/21/follow-the-leadership-spending/ [accessed 14 January 2022].

Skillings, P. (2008) *Escape from Corporate America*. New York: Ballantine Books.

Thunnissen, M., Boselie, P. and Fruytier, B. (2013) Talent management and the relevance of context: Towards a pluralistic approach, *Human Resource Management Review*, 23(4): 326–36.

Wall, T., Iordanou, I., Hawley, R. and Csigás, Z. (eds) (2016) *Research Policy and Practice Provocations: Bridging the Gap – Towards Research that Sparks and Connects Coaches in Research and Practice*. Brussels: European Mentoring and Coaching Council.

Wall, T., Jamieson, M., Csigás, Z. and Kiss, O. (eds) (2017) *Research Policy and Practice Provocations: Coaching Evaluation in Diverse Landscapes of Practice – Towards Enriching Toolkits and Professional Judgement*. Brussels: European Mentoring and Coaching Council.

Wright, P. and McMahan, G. (2011) Exploring human capital: Putting 'human' back into strategic human resource management, *Human Resource Management Journal*, 21(2): 93–104.

Yapp, M. (2009) Measuring the ROI of talent management, *Strategic HR Review*, 8(4): 5–10.

Index

Page numbers in italics are figures; with 't' are tables.